the
high
school

survival guide

All you need to know in order to get through high school alive **and keep your friends beside you, written by teenagers (and one awesome adult!) who've done it themselves.**

First published 2011 by MoshPit Publishing
an imprint of Mosher's Business Support Pty Ltd
Shop 1, 197 Great Western Highway, Hazelbrook NSW 2779
Email: books@moshpitpublishing.com.au
Website: www.moshpitpublishing.com.au

First edition
Copyright © Ally Mosher 2011

The moral rights of the author have been asserted.

National Library of Australia Cataloguing-in-Publication data:

Author:	Mosher, Ally, 1991-
Contributors:	Keith, Tracy; Phillips, Darren; and Francis, Ben
Title:	The High School Survival Guide: a handbook for the modern teenage girl
ISBN:	978-0-9871731-5-7 (paperback)
	978-0-9871731-6-4 (ebook)
Subjects:	Mind and Body, Interpersonal Relations

Editing and Proofreading: Jennifer Mosher AE
Photography: Darren Phillips (except for final image of Jasmine and Polly, Ben Francis and Tracy Keith, which were used with permission, and image of Darren Phillips, which was taken by Jennifer Mosher.)
Layout and design: Ally Mosher

the
high
school
survival guide

Written by Ally Mosher,
Ben 'R-Tizt' Francis
and Tracy Keith of TMK Consulting

Photography by Darren Phillips of Darphi Images

Makeup by Jasmine Lovelock-Dorfler

Modelled for by fourteen fun, mature and confident
teenagers from the Blue Mountains, NSW, Australia
(see back of book for bios)

This book is dedicated to

all the wonderful friends I had in high school
who patiently forgave all my social errors
and helped me work out who I was,

and with so much love
to my beautiful sister
Sara Mosher
who has been a fiercely loyal best friend,
and to whom I owe so much.

intro

Are you a parent? Turn to page 157.

Hi—I'm Ally, and I've finished high school. Yes, I'm still alive, and I'm still sane, which means you can get there too. Sometimes things we go through in high school are just because we're teenagers—other times it's because we're at school. Either way, they're all situations that (with a little bit of help), we can make the most of and get through with our dignity and sanity intact.

I'm no expert, and I won't pretend to be, but all the way through high school I was wishing I had a survival guide. So when I graduated, I thought 'I've got a year off, why not write one?'

Because I'm no expert, I've talked to New Zealand careers expert Tracy Keith who brings you some killer career advice in the worklife section, and singer/dancer/actor Ben Francis in England for the (surprising!) secrets of how guys think.

Nonetheless, everything in here is just advice, so make sure you adjust it to your own situation! All I can do is tell you what I did in my circumstances. Yours may be different. Solving problems our own way and learning from our mistakes is how we get to be world-savvy women who can take on any challenge (and look damn good doing it)!

I've packed this book full of study advice because that's definitely the worst part about high school. It's not just about exams, though. This book will help you with family life, friends, dating, how you view yourself, even getting a job. All the things that most teenagers achieve in their time at high school, really. And you'll achieve a lot! Make the most of it and be proud of yourself when you graduate. And pass on your wisdom to others, too! You'll be surprised how far you've come. And hopefully I can help you with that.

contents

contents

contents

contents

school
life

High school can get a little crazy. You're balancing work, friends, teachers you might not like, you probably hate, and all the while trying to find time to sleep. Here's the run down on making decisions at school that will benefit you for your whole life.

Starting all over ...

It's a bit of an anticlimax to finish primary school feeling all big and mature, and then be thrown straight into high school where you're the youngest. Again. The smallest. Again. Brand new. All over again. But every older student was a newbie in high school once, and they all survived! Just follow these tips and you'll love high school in no time.

Making friends

Remember firstly that the way people seem to be is very rarely the way they actually are.

Some people are rude when they're nervous. Try to see past it—laugh a lot while you're talking to them, smile, be friendly. It won't take them long to calm down and start being nice.

Don't judge people too quickly! That timid girl from a rival primary school might be your best friend by the end of the month. Take your chances. Meet as many new students as you can.

Join any cross-grade groups such as Rock Eisteddfod or the Student Representative Council if you want friends in older grades. These help in getting an idea of the way the school works, and with friends in older grades you'll have more influence.

Be yourself. You might think you're acting 'cool', but everyone else might be seeing you as a total bitch. If you're just who you are, then the friends you make now will be your true friends; they'll like you for you, not who you're trying to be.

Classmates can be great first friends. Try to sit with different people in each subject, but keep it the same per lesson so that you'll get to know your desk buddies.

Stuck for conversation? Compare timetables, ask about the canteen menu, see if they play any sport or like drama. Ask them about themselves and you'll be deep in conversation in no time.

Don't try too hard. That may sound backwards but if you're making too much of an effort you'll come off as clingy. Just relax! You WILL make friends.

Student politics
Modesty and maturity are key!

In this first week, you have to rein in all your primary school leader attitude and basically just accept that you're at the bottom of the food chain again. But only for a while! Because while high school politics unfortunately exist, if you prove yourself worthy, you can overcome the 'newbie' label and just be known as the cool person that you are!

Try these tips:

- Don't try to sit at the back of the bus. Sit with a friend, and don't talk too loudly. In time, you can move towards the back without some idiot older student claiming it's his seat, but for now, just sit where you can!

Try to sit with different people in each subject. You'll soon get to know your desk buddies.

- Your uniform should be neat and pretty generic in the first few weeks. This will make it easier for students to get to know you, too—if you dress slutty or punk on the first day, that label will be slapped on you for life. Don't give anybody a reason to judge you too quickly!
- Follow the rules. Don't stand in the walkways chatting, don't cut into the canteen line. Older students are often under a lot of study stress and will snap quickly if you get in their way.
- Find a spot for your group in the playground and stay there. By keeping your group in a fixed position you're claiming your area—you might even have it until graduation!
- If older students speak to you, look them in the eye and reply honestly. Don't take anything they say personally, and don't overreact or get angry—they're testing you, and if you respond maturely, laugh, or even make them laugh, you've passed.

New classes

Get a head start, even in Term 1.

You'll figure out pretty quickly which classes you like and which you don't. Hopefully you can change teachers next year, and subjects soon, and it won't matter. Regardless, keep ahead of the crowd with the following tips:

- Do your homework! It'll set you up for good marks in later years.
- Ask questions and contribute to the conversation, but don't whisper to your friends or distract the class.
- Rephrase what the teacher is saying in your head to help the ideas really sink in. Don't be afraid to ask if you don't understand!

The study solution

You need to learn your work if you want to do well. But when you get home in the afternoon there are probably a million other things you'd rather be doing than hitting the books! It's understandable. And it's internationally agreed: study sucks. However, once you decide you need to get it done, there are quite a few tricks you can use to try to make it easier. Here are some of the best solutions to the study problem.

you need:

If your study area has the following things, you'll do much better:

- highlighters
- stapler
- tape
- hole punch
- binder folders
- pens and pencils
- desk lamp
- dictionary
- sticky notes and tabs
- system cards
- blank paper (not lined)
- lined paper
- ruler
- calculator

mind tricks

Don't procrastinate—start studying the minute you get home. Throw together a quick afternoon tea and eat it while you hit the books. This keeps you in school mode and you can stop studying early in the evening and enjoy your dinner guilt-free! You'll soon get into the habit of studying straight away: your mind will link the two and you'll stop feeling like you're missing out.

If you don't feel like studying, just grab some notes and read them. Just chill out on a couch and read. Read quietly, out loud, or even sing. It's lazy, yes, but you'll still absorb some knowledge.

Do what you want *after* a good study session, like watching TV or taking a bath. You deserve it!

systematic

System cards (large lined palm cards) are so useful for summaries. It's a psychological trick: a handful of cards summarising an entire year's work is so much less scary than an entire binder folder!

Also, the size of the cards will force you to summarise, and consider what you really need to know, and what you don't. Keep it simple and try to use one card or less for each concept. Write headings and important points in red and use diagrams if you learn visually.

The best bit is that they're portable. Study on the bus, at breakfast, even in the bath!

get visual

If piles of notes scare you, make a mind map. Draw pictures and diagrams that help you remember.

Start with the heading in the middle, branch out to subheadings, put definitions in red and highlight important points. Make sure you number your mind maps so you know the order. You could even colour-code your mind maps using a different colour paper for each subject.

Stick the mind maps on your wall and they'll sink in before you know it—come exam time, all you need to do is picture the mind map and it'll come right back to you!

multi task

Like to watch TV or work out, but no longer have time? You can do it all if you do it all at once. Study with afternoon tea in front of the telly, or record yourself speaking and listen to it while you walk the dog or go for a run.

By laminating your notes you can even study in the bath or shower. Leave a textbook on the kitchen bench overnight to remind you to study with breakfast. Take notes on palm cards to read on the bus.

If you're musical, why not write a song from your notes? Maths equations are easier to remember when they rhyme!

Get creative! There are loads of ways you can multi-task.

the goal

So, you want an overall score of 80? Achievable. Get a piece of coloured card and write on it with permanent marker. Keep it simple, like 'mark: 80 or over' or 'final mark: 75'. Stick it to a wall near your study area. If you use a computer to study, make it your desktop background. Just make it an achievable goal.

Stick it on your binder folder that you take to school. It doesn't have to be big or pretty; it just has to be somewhere that you'll see it all the time. It'll motivate you every time you look at it.

And make sure you reward yourself for reaching that goal! Buy yourself a gift, or celebrate somehow. It might be new shoes, a sleepover or even a cake for yourself! Just make it something worth working towards.

ADAPT AND IMPROVE:
handling criticism

Everyone knows how it feels. Your pride and joy, that essay you thought you absolutely nailed ... returned to you covered in red. Suggestions, crosses, spelling errors. All you want to do is trash it on the way out of the classroom and never think about it again, but it's far more beneficial to put yourself through looking at the marks and asking why. Here's how to handle it when the teacher's been harsh.

Firstly, if you're not good with criticism, don't look at the paper in front of your friends! It's more embarrassing than it's worth, and you might end up just dismissing the teacher as an idiot and wasting all that valuable advice. Wait until you're at home, and preferably alone—prepare yourself, and take your time reading over it.

Remember! Your teacher isn't trying to hurt your feelings. If they didn't care about your work you'd just have FAIL and nothing else. Your teacher has sat down for hours giving his or her students good advice—it's worth reading it all in a friendly tone and learning from it.

Go through the essay, noting each piece of advice. Think about each individually—ask yourself 'is this good advice? Where can I implement this in future essays?' Avoid being cruel to yourself with thoughts like 'I really should have thought of that' or 'I'm so dumb'. You're at school to learn, and if you were already perfect at everything, school would be a waste, wouldn't it?

From here you have three options:
1. Accept the advice, file or trash the assignment, and use your new knowledge for your next assignment.
2. Rewrite the essay or redo the assignment and

ask your teacher to check and see if you've understood his or her advice correctly.

3. Argue the advice. Perhaps the teacher has misunderstood you, or if you feel the criticism is destructive, say so, but politely. Say to your teacher, 'Here you've written "this could be better" but you haven't said how. Could you give me some constructive criticism please?' This will help them realise that their negative notes aren't helping anybody and they'll try harder next time to give you suggestions, rather than just shutting you down.

You can avoid written criticism by just not reading your essays, but you'll never really improve if you don't take advice. It's more of a matter of deciding which advice to accept and what to reject, rather than just rejecting it all. Try not to take it personally! Of course, that's easily said about written criticism—but what if it's **face-to-face**? Generally, everybody hates being told off, and generally it feels worse when you know you deserve it. We all react different ways—some people laugh and pretend they don't care, others cry or get angry. Wouldn't it be awesome if you were able to just take it and move on? With a little practice, you'll be brilliant at it. Here's how to handle face-to-face criticism—in this case, it's about an essay:

1. Take a very long, slooooow, deep breath. Breathe in, hold it there, breathe out. Resist the urge to interrupt the speaker or reply without thought.
2. Make eye contact with the speaker. Listen to what they're saying, and even wait a few seconds at the end—to make sure they're done speaking and to calm yourself down. It often makes the speaker a bit nervous if you look at them and smile a little when they're done—this is a good way to level the playing field if they've been harsh.
3. Preface ANYTHING you say with 'Thanks for being honest with me. I appreciate your opinion.' This will set the speaker off guard—they're probably preparing to defend their position so they'll appreciate that you can hear their point of view.

4. Regardless of whether you agree or disagree, say 'I'll think about what you said.' You might be required to say 'I'll think about what you said and get back to you' if their criticism needs a response, but otherwise, leave the conversation at that. Turn it to other things, or walk away. Be calm and polite, even if you're faking it.
5. Think about what they've said when you're alone. Resist the urge to mull over the way they've said it ('I can't believe she said I was lazy!') and instead think about the underlying message ('She's saying she thinks I'd do well if I try harder.')
6. Do you agree with the underlying message? If you do, approach the speaker later and let them know ('I had a think about what you said. Do you have any extra worksheets I could have a look at for this assignment?').
7. If you don't agree, say why, calmly, and back it up with a rational argument. ('I thought about what you said, but I think you might be overestimating me. I did try really hard at that assignment and I'm proud of my work. I don't feel I was lazy with this; maybe I just didn't understand the assignment.')
8. Either way, you might not like what you hear, but don't try to start an argument! Best case scenario, you'll sort it out calmly with mutual benefit, and you'll both be impressed with the negotiating skills you've each displayed. If the teacher gets defensive, back yourself up with 'I'll give you some time to think about what I've said—shall we talk about it tomorrow?' to give them a chance to collect their thoughts.
9. If the teacher really isn't interested in giving you more useful feedback—take it to another teacher instead. You never know, a second opinion might lead to a better mark!

THE MYTH OF

Popularity

POPULARITY:

n. the quality of being widely admired or accepted or sought after

Popularity—one of the most enduring myths of modern-day society. It's absolute crap: if there's true popularity anywhere, it's not what we're thinking of. Think of the 'popular' group at your high school. Most likely, in this world so affected by music and movies, you're thinking of a group of girls in short skirts that don't ever get involved in any school activities, and find amazing ways to make the school uniform slutty. They wear too much makeup, they abuse the colour pink, and they chew gum, especially when they shouldn't. They use the term 'loser' and they talk about nothing more than boys and bitches. 'Mean Girls' type stuff.

They might have guys in their group—tall, sporty, pants too low, egos too inflated. They're always threatening to beat people up and they talk loudly about their latest sexual conquests. They might be smart, but they hide it—they'd rather smoke and wag class because they think they're cooler that way.

Now, compare the definition of 'popular' with this group. It doesn't match, does it? Nobody admires these people. Nobody accepts them, and not many people seek them out. They're hated, gossiped about, and avoided when possible. They make you feel inadequate, but the truth is, they're the losers! Your grade or school might have a group like this, and don't they just make you feel so uncomfortable? That's not popularity.

If you had to say who you thought was really popular, wouldn't you end up choosing who had the most friends, those who are widely accepted and sought after, people who fit perfectly into any group and who know the names of everybody? People who everybody knows! People who will always make you laugh. People who will party with absolutely anyone.

They're popular because they're not mean, they're not fake, and they're not exclusive. The stereotypical 'popular' people won't talk to anyone outside their group unless they want something. You know what happens to those groups? There'll be between three and eight of them, normally—and on an excursion day, or near the end of term, one of them will find themselves at school, alone, with nobody else to talk to.

The real popular people never have that problem. When their resident group isn't there, there's always another group happy to take them in for the day.

Be yourself, and don't bother sucking up to the 'popular' girls, because all you'll get out of that is an inability to accept yourself, a hatred of how inadequate you feel around them, and absolutely NO real friends.

Join a group that talks about life and parties and school—not just boys and bitches. Join a group that laughs a lot, and doesn't spend hours choosing clothes and makeup. Join a group that never shuts you out, and catches you up on the conversation each morning when you arrive at school. Because, when you all graduate, the 'popular' girls will find that their bitchy exclusive approach will fail miserably in the real world, and they'll be painfully alone, like the 'losers' they once made fun of. And you? You'll be confident, happy, you will have had a blast at high school, and people will WANT to talk to you. You'll meet thousands of people in your life; why shut a single person out? Find a group that makes you feel good about yourself, and your social skills, your schoolwork, what you do on the weekends, how you feel about yourself, all of it, will instantly be so much better.

> I ain't gonna lie, I never really liked school. I would sit in class and do my artwork or beat box. At break time I would go and dance or free run. My school was troublesome at times; fights occasionally took part without the teachers finding out—I didn't get into any though. I used to hate non uniform [mufti] day because my clothes were rubbish, apart from the very last day.
>
> I came in all white—I plaited my hair with white beads, I had a white New Era hat on, a white Lyle and Scott jacket, my dungarees and my white Air Forces. As a senior I used to always wear trainers to school even though you weren't meant to, and different jackets but coming to mufti

ben says

day that day, I wanted to stand out—and yes, I do believe some people were shocked, because that's the day you get to show what you really dress like outside of school and that day always seems so laid back.

A lot of people don't follow school rules that day, you just feel free. But it's good that non uniform only happens once in a while because it's the one day when students can get bullied a lot about their dress sense. I experienced this on non uniform day from years 7—9. But its all good now—I'm now known as the swagga kid! [the guy with great style]

Don't be a Victim:

beating the bullies

If you're lucky, you'll go through your entire high school years without being bullied. But if you do find someone targets you, first remember that it's not your fault. A lot of bullying victims have no idea what they did to gain the bully's attention, and that's just it: you didn't do anything. It's not your fault, and you deserve better. Luckily in this day and age you don't have to suffer silently.

You are in Control

When somebody is picking on you, it might feel like there's nothing you can do about it. True, you don't have control over their actions, but you can control your reactions. Take their power away by listening to yourself instead.

Next time they say something to you, smile to yourself. Take deep breaths and concentrate on slowing your pulse. Say to yourself that their insults aren't true. And believe it! The most poisonous part of being a victim of bullying is not the bully itself, it's when you start believing what the bully is saying. Think about it rationally—they barely know you! It's not up to them to decide if you're fat, ugly, or a loser. You know you're not. And even if you are overweight or not 'cool', who cares? You might have a great sense of humour, or you're smart, or you could be great at a sport or hobby. You're real, with flaws and strengths.

You don't have nothing. **You are not nothing.** Don't believe a word they say because they do not know you, like you know yourself. Why let their opinions bother you? **You know who you are!**

They're wrong, and the reason that bitch is trying to make you hate yourself, is because she hates *her*self! Maybe she's jealous of how confident you are, when she can barely look in the mirror. You're stronger than her—*you* don't need to victimise other people to get your kicks. You are the winner.

And you are in control of your own thoughts and opinions. Use them!

Asking for Help is Okay

Never, under any circumstances, feel that you can't go and see somebody for help. Teachers, the school counsellor, your parents or guardians, friends or an older sibling are all there to help you. And so are the police. If the bullying gets to an extreme state, the police can help.

Keep a diary. Write down what the bully said or did on each day: where you were, who witnessed it, what was said and when. Try to gather as many witnesses as you can. If you feel you can handle It on your own, do so, but if it gets to the stage where the stress is interfering with your life, go and talk to somebody. All schools these days should have anti-bullying policies in place: use them! Those rules are there because you're not the only person who has found themselves in this situation: and most people find their way out of the issue, as well. You're not alone and the teachers can help. Take the diary to a teacher and tell them as much as you can about the situation. Set up a code with the teacher if you're worried the bully will realise you've been talking to them. For example, the teacher might ask you to stay back after class to talk about your assignment, and that can be code for talking about the bully.

Phone and Cyber Bullying

Cyber bullying (and bullying by SMS) is ridiculously

stupid, because it leaves you with proof of every single thing the bully has said, every threat they have made. Save everything to your computer. Take screenshots of each comment the minute it appears (or copy and paste—or both) and keep a record of the date and time of each comment. If you reply, keep a record of that too, but don't try to bully back!

Any public threat made against you is an offence worth going to the police for. If the bully posts on your social profile that 'you're dead' or that they'll 'bash you tomorrow', you've got enough to go to the police on. It helps to talk to an adult first before taking it straight to the police, and they can help you put together your complaint.

One thing to remember: don't threaten them back! Comments like 'please leave me alone' are fine, and insults that aren't threatening, while not ideal, are sometimes necessary, but NEVER make a public threat against your bully—because then they have a case against you, too.

If you feel safe enough, say to your cyber bully to please stop commenting you or you'll go to the police. Keep a record of when you made this comment and the response. The idea alone might be enough to deter your bully, but if they continue, you know you gave them a chance to stop.

Challenge their Motives

In many circumstances you won't get a safe chance to ask this question, but in some cases it can start a conversation that leads to the end of your problems. If the bully is a cyber bully, or if you're certain that they aren't going to physically hurt you, ask them why. Say 'What did I do to make you so angry?' or 'Why are you being so mean?'

Say it calmly—instead of yelling it. Seriously ask the question as though you're curious about the answer. You may not get a real response from the bully, but it will definitely stick in their mind and might just lead to a change in their ways, depending on the level of the bullying.

Keep Yourself Social

During this time you're likely to feel alone and very stressed—normal responses to a difficult situation. But this doesn't mean you *are* alone, and it definitely doesn't mean you're not loved! Combat this feeling by surrounding yourself with friends and family. If you feel like you have no friends, join a class or group after school to meet some new people. Even spend some quality time with the family pet or your neighbours. It doesn't matter who they are, as long as they're nice to you! Even if they don't know about the bullying, their friendship will be your support during this period.

Is she a bully . . . or just a bitch?

She stole your pen and so you reported her for bullying. You might have all the support in the world at first, until the Principal sits you down and asks you to describe exactly what she did to bully you. When he finds out it was a one-off encounter where she decided to keep a 60 cent pen, he'll probably be less than receptive to your pleas!

Learn the difference between bitches and bullies. A one-off nasty comment might just be a normally nice girl having a really bad day. It probably has nothing to do with you.

However, if she seeks you out to insult or hurt you and it happens repeatedly and in a similar fashion each time, then it's bullying. And if the bullying is physical—if you are being beat up—see someone about it immediately. Even if it's happened once. If somebody seeks you out with the main aim being to hurt you: tell a teacher straight away.

Get Smarter without Trying!

9 EASY WAYS TO IMPROVE YOUR BRAIN

Guess what? 'Nerds' are just normal people with natural smarts. They might enjoy school more, true, but that's because they're good at it. Don't you enjoy what you're good at, too?

Now you know that little secret, here's another: you can tune your brain to be better at school too. And there are easy ways to do it. Read on! (Reading's one—you're already helping yourself. See how easy?!!)

1 Read a Newspaper

Most common newspapers have a reading age of about 10. You can do it! Sit with a dictionary next to you if you want, and only read articles that look interesting. You don't have to read the whole thing.

Benefits: your reading and knowledge of world events, business and politics will get better, as will your powers of argument if you discuss what you've read.

2 Do Word Puzzles

Calm down, you're not a nerd if you do puzzles! Find a celebrity-related or pop culture crossword and give it a shot. Try logic puzzles, Sudoku (it's pretty trendy) or word jumbles. Most of these can be found in your daily paper, or online.

Benefits: your spelling and logic skills will get better, both which lead to better marks at school. And the sense of achievement when you finish a killer Sudoku is great.

3 Talk to Adults

Sounds snooty, but talking to your friends' parents and other adults can really help build your conversational skills. Talk about anything, but really listen!

Benefits: your vocabulary will grow without you even knowing it, and you'll build the ability to change your language based on your audience: it's really important in essay writing.

4 Change Channels

Trashy TV is all well and good, but just once or twice a week, switch over and watch a documentary. Pick something you're interested in, like sport or architecture, then sit back, relax, and reap the benefits!

Benefits: you get to watch an interesting TV show, learn about something that interests you, build your vocabulary and you'll probably pick up some good facts for future assignments.

5 Coming home from a mentally exhausting school day and getting straight down to homework can really kill your brain. Refresh yourself by getting some exercise in the open air: walk the dog, play a sport or even just work out inside with the windows open. When you sit down to study you'll find your mind is clearer and you can focus.

Benefits: your brain will work better! Fresh air and exercise are great to refresh yourself, increase your ability to focus, and boost motivation. If it's raining, why not do yoga on the balcony?

6 Argue

Find a topic you're passionate about and have a (friendly!) debate with a friend or family member. Make sure you're well-researched though, and be open to hearing their opinions!

Benefits: your vocabulary and debating skills will get a boost and you'll learn—you'll learn by listening to the other side of the argument, and you'll learn to accept other opinions!

7 Learn to Listen

Class is easier if you're actually hearing the teacher. Try repeating everything they say in your head for it to really sink in.

Benefits: school will be easier! You'll have learnt more in class, so study will be simpler and you'll do better in assignments.

8 Audition for a Play

Learn a monologue and perform it at an audition. You might get the part; even if you don't you've benefited from it!

Benefits: your memory will improve from learning the audition piece, and will continue to improve if you get a part and have to learn directions and lines. You'll also learn public speaking and voice skills which definitely come in handy in English, Drama and job interviews.

9 Go to Bed

Get some sleep. Nothing can be a simpler get-smart method than that!

Benefits: you wake up sharper and ready to learn. You're more likely to focus, more likely to be cheerful and you'll gain a valuable boost in motivation and energy!

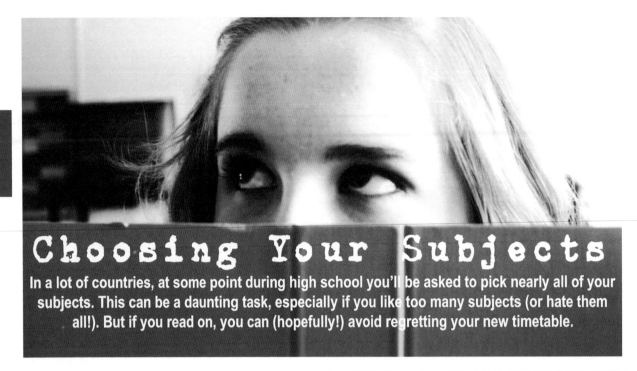

Choosing Your Subjects

In a lot of countries, at some point during high school you'll be asked to pick nearly all of your subjects. This can be a daunting task, especially if you like too many subjects (or hate them all!). But if you read on, you can (hopefully!) avoid regretting your new timetable.

Pick subjects you're interested in or think you'll enjoy. No point taking Physics (unless you need it for your career) if you know you don't really like it—your marks will drop if you're not interested, and you'd do better in a subject you like.

Don't pick subjects **just because your friends are taking them.** Sometimes it's exciting to be in a class of strangers. You'll make new friends and you'll do better at the subject without the distractions.

Choose subjects you're good at. If you have a knack for HTML, maximise your marks with Computer Studies.

Consider the teacher you're likely to have. If the only Drama teacher is a total idiot, think seriously about whether you could handle being taught by them for two years. There are always other schools.

If you know **what you want to do as a job,** consider what subjects would help you get there. If you want to be a scientist, is Modern History really a good choice over Biology?

Trust your instincts. If you 'just have a really good feeling' about Dance, it can't hurt to follow that feeling, right? Remember, there's always a chance you can change if you realise early on that you've made a mistake.

Write lists. Try different combinations of subjects and see how they go together.

Talk about it! Your friends and parents might have an interesting insight on a certain subject or combination. Also, talk to older students who took the subject—they'll be able to warn you if it's particularly stressful or boring!

Set preferences. In case of a subject clash, it helps to think beforehand over which topics you *really* want to study and which ones you could live without.

Don't stress—your subjects at high school don't determine your entire future! And you won't be pigeonholed into admin jobs if you take Business Studies, or IT jobs if you take Computer Studies. Your career is your choice.

Opportunities and Clubs

Think clubs are lame? Would you say that if you knew they could get you a better job?

When you graduate high school, you may not have much on your resume for work. You may have had one or two casual jobs, and your graduation marks, but most people your age will have these things to offer as well.

If you want to get a better job straight out of school, you need to stand out. And to stand out, the best way is to develop your skills by making the most of opportunities in school.

No matter what it is you get involved with, seeing volunteer involvement on your resume will impress any employer. It says to an employer that you work hard and you're willing to do more than you need to. And really, who wouldn't want to hire somebody like that?

SPORT

Whether it's soccer or swimming, sport's a CV gem. Being in a team shows you can work with others towards a common goal: exactly what companies do. You're committed, and you take time out of your life for others. You may also be at a good level of fitness: perfect for outdoors jobs. And any sport leadership role is definitely worth listing. Teamwork's so important for a job!

DEBATING

Strangely, knowing how to argue is a damn good skill. Debating shows public speaking skills, good writing and arguing skills, logical thinking, teamwork, determination, and good presentation. It means you're trusted to represent your school. It's irrelevant if you won—you have skills, and you'll be able to confidently make presentations or speak to customers at your new job!

SRC

SRC (Student Rep Council) will make you a manager! SRC shows that you're willing to go the extra mile to improve the place you're in. As an ambassador of the school you'll learn leadership, teamwork and public speaking skills, as well as commitment and the ability to manage and organise events, even delegating tasks. All of these skills are vital for a management position and will look really good on your resume, especially if you end up as a School Captain!

DRAMA CLUB

Not only do you get to be in plays, drama club gives you some really job-worthy skills. Teamwork, commitment, good public speaking skills, clear strong voice, good projection— these are just the start of skills you can list on your resume from any drama class. And any employer will be pleased to see that you have the confidence to perform: confidence in a customer-service role is really useful and drama shows you have a good memory, can take direction, and learn fast.

CHARITY

Especially useful when going for scholarships, charity work shows you care deeply for others. Organised a great fundraiser for Amnesty? Always been an ambassador for the Blood Drive? Great! List it. Any kind of charity shows you're passionate and committed to a cause. Employers will see that you have the determination to go that extra mile and help others. Great when going for scholarships and leadership jobs—charity work shows you care about your community.

Can't figure out why your teacher keeps calling you by the wrong name, yelling at you for nothing, or expecting you to laugh at his awkward jokes? Read on.

FORGETS YOUR NAME

'My name is Jenna, not Anna!' Drill it into their heads.

It's difficult to do, but you need to correct them every time they get your name wrong. Be polite, especially if they're confusing you with a relative. Say 'It's okay, it happens all the time!' and laugh, but make sure they've heard your actual name. Write it clearly on every paper you submit; even every page. Keep it in their heads as much as you can.

If they keep calling you that, try 'forgetting' their name a few times. They'll soon try harder when they know how it feels!

OVERENTHUSIASTIC

Love for the subject is a good thing for a teacher to have. But it's hard to be patient if you hate what they're teaching!

Firstly, teachers are people. Try not to offend him/her by groaning every time they suggest an activity—the more excited they are, the more likely you could really offend them.

If you really need your teacher to dial it down, try approaching them before a lesson and politely saying, 'I have a headache but I didn't want to miss class. Is there any chance we could just quietly take notes today?' They'll be pleased at your commitment, and might just reward you.

MAKES BAD JOKES

If he makes lame jokes and always looks at you for laughter, it can be hard to be nice but not a suck-up.

If the joke's funny, laugh! Others will probably join in. And if they don't, try not to be embarrassed.

If it's not funny but he's looking at you for support, smile and give a small nod. Hopefully it will be enough.

If it's racist or offensive, avoid eye contact and look shocked. Hopefully he'll realise that if you were offended, the whole class might be!

HARD MARKER

Another C- and no idea why? These teachers are frustrating, but communication helps.

If they're always marking you down but never giving comments, pull them up on it. After class, approach them and say 'I really don't know how I lost so many marks, can you please go through this with me and show me where I could improve?' If they see you're depressed at your mark but are willing to improve, not only will they be clearer with comments but might mark you higher to encourage you next time.

If your friend wrote similar responses and got a better mark, take their work too, to compare. It might help back up your case.

If you really think you deserved better, you could quietly take it to another teacher for marking, but be careful! Use this as a last resort.

Surviving Exams

You can laugh about them, cry about them, try to avoid them ... but in the end, every high school student will have to sit exams. But don't worry too much—it's all about preparation, and with the right plan you'll breeze through the finals and barely stress at all!

Even if you aren't the type to stress out, you probably aren't looking forward to the exams. The most important thing to remember is that exams aren't a competition, and they're not the be all and end all of school. The point of an exam is to test how well you've learnt each year. Think of it like a science experiment: they have to put all the students in the same conditions so that the marks actually mean something.

It's not about cramming the night before. Exams will be a breeze with a little preparation. Here are the best things to remember while you're studying and coming up to your exams:

Most students underestimate the importance of a good night's sleep. Do whatever you have to do to make that bed a haven—don't study or eat in bed because you'll then relate your bed to those activities and not for sleeping. Set the alarm 10 minutes later where you can, and nap during the afternoon if you have to. You don't have to sacrifice your social life, necessarily, but sometimes it's wise to have a Friday night in watching TV in your pyjamas instead of out at a party with your friends. Even if you feel you should be doing schoolwork, it's important to schedule *some* time for yourself every now and then.

Max your study in minimum time

Incidental study works wonders. Use sticky notes, paper, palm cards—anything to jog your memory. Write facts and syllabus points on them and stick them around the house. Make a study book to flick through while you're watching TV. Use a diagram as your computer wallpaper. If you're always sort of studying, it'll sink in much faster than you might expect.

Schedule actual study sessions as well as incidental study. Make a routine—for example, each day after school, you come home, check the mail, do your chores, make afternoon tea, and sit down to study. Don't give yourself a chance to turn on the television. If you study from 4pm to 5:30pm, you'll have the whole afternoon after that to do whatever you want. You'll enjoy watching TV more when you've done the study for the day, rather than thinking 'I should really stop watching this and study' every five minutes!

If you really can't get yourself into the habit, try studying with food, while exercising (yes, it can be done!), while listening to music, or even in front of the TV. Get yourself into the habit of studying each afternoon, and eventually you'll find you don't need the distraction anymore.

Schedules sound nerdy but they really do help. If you've got your finals coming up and you're studying for everything at once, draw your afternoon up into a schedule so that each subject gets equal time across the week. Stick the schedule to the wall or in your diary so you see it every day, and take the chance to feel good about yourself when you stick to the schedule. It can be as detailed as time slots, or as general as day-to-day subject allocations, such as the following schedule example:

Monday—Maths, Biology
Tuesday—Drama, History
Wednesday—English, Maths
Thursday—Biology, Drama
Friday—History, rest of the afternoon off.

Make sure you have time to do homework and assignments as well as study!

You'll develop your own study tricks, comfort kit (see the opposite page) and ways to get through your exams with sanity intact. If it works for you—even if it's singing your notes!—then do it. Nobody needs to know what your study habits are, so long as you're learning.

On the Day

The morning of the exam is always an unpleasant one. Unpleasant at best, awful at worst. Try these tricks to make it easier:

- The day before, set your alarm an hour early, so you're tired when you go to bed. This will keep you from lying awake too long and worrying about the next day. Try to cut down on your sugar intake the day before as well.
- On the morning of the exam, have an iron-rich breakfast with carbs (such as eggs or baked beans on toast) for energy that will last during the day.
- On the bus or train to the exam, refresh yourself with your notes. Try not to worry too much, just read over the notes and see how you go.
- Treat yourself to a small bar of chocolate in the hour leading up to the exam.
- If you're feeling nervous, close your eyes and concentrate on breathing. Stand with your feet shoulder-width apart (or if you're sitting, uncross your legs) and take deep breaths in through the nose, all the way to your stomach, and breathe out slowly through your mouth.

Questions answered: 6.
Pens chewed: 20!

- Just relax! Keep it in perspective. You'll do your best, and nobody can ask any more of you than that.

In the Exam

Even once you're in the room, there are tricks you can use to make it easier. Once you learn how to make the most of your time in the exam room, you'll breeze through the tests with no worries.

- When you get the exam paper, you're usually given 5-10 minutes to read. USE IT! Read through the whole exam. Get an idea for what you might say in the extended response, and if there's multiple choice, use the time to figure out the first three or four answers so you can get a head start when writing begins.

- If you've got an exam referencing multiple electives or texts and you have to trawl through to find your pages, turn the top corner of the page down—or tear it off altogether—to make it easier to find each question when the writing time starts.

- If your hand is getting sore, put the pen down and shake it for two or three seconds. After shaking it, make a fist and then stretch your hand out a few times. If you need to, just rest it completely still on the desk for fifteen seconds or so. Relaxing the muscles will give you the energy you need to pick that pen back up and finish the essay.

- Wear very comfortable clothes to the exams. If you have to wear uniform, wear looser clothes than normal and wear comfortable shoes.

- Use scrap paper. If you have a mental blank,

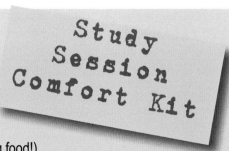

Study Session Comfort Kit

- Loose, comfortable trackpants or pyjama pants
- Slippers
- A big jumper or soft dressing gown
- Herbal tea (or other yummy calming drink)
- Chewing gum (to keep you from procrastinating by making food!)
- Muesli bars (or other quick snacks, for the same reason)
- Scented candles (put them out before you leave the room!)
- Lavender oil (rub it into your temples [if it's skin-friendly!] to soothe a headache)

think 'what do I know about this subject?'—even if it's not relevant to the question—and just write it all down. Eventually you'll come to something you can use.

- If you're not sure of an answer, don't leave the space blank! There's nothing wrong with guessing. You might get half-marks (or full marks—you might be right!) if you guess, but if you leave it blank you don't even have a chance of a mark. It doesn't matter if your answer makes you look like an idiot. Just write something!

- If a question is really confusing you, mark the margin next to it with an asterisk and move on. If you finish the exam with time to spare, come back to it and give it another shot. If you run out of time, it's better that you spent the time writing answers to questions, rather than staring at the ones that confuse you! If you're really stuck, just come back to it later.

- It's easy to get sullen if you think you're doing badly in an exam. You might start to hate yourself and think 'I'm stupid, I can't finish this'. Stop that now! You'll only do badly if you think like that. Just think 'This is a hard exam, but I know my work' and keep going. Better yet, don't give yourself time to think at all. You shouldn't be evaluating your performance during the exam. Just do it! Worry about it afterwards. You'll do better if you don't think like that at all.

After the Exam

Congratulations! No matter how good or bad it was, the exam is over. They all end eventually! Go home—rest, relax, reward yourself. Watch TV aimlessly, sleep, eat chocolate. Recycle your study notes (if you won't need them later!!). Allow yourself to feel good, because you have achieved something! It's a challenge, with a goal, and now it's over. Enjoy the feeling.

If you have more exams coming up, study according to what motivates you most. You might need a break first, and then get some notes out in the afternoon. Or, if you know that a break will mean you basically don't study at all, throw yourself into the next subject the minute you can. Either way, don't forget to eat, drink lots of water, and relax! Stay in good health during the exam period—there's nothing worse than a sore throat or runny nose distracting you from the exam.

Whatever you do for the rest of the day, don't stress or think too much about particular answers. You can't change the past, and you might still get half marks, even if you really screwed up a response. Everyone will have made a mistake somewhere, so try not to worry, and don't be too harsh on yourself! You sat the exam, you tried your hardest, and that in itself is an awesome achievement. Nice work!

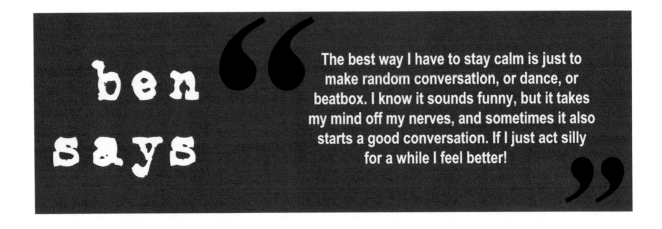

ben says

The best way I have to stay calm is just to make random conversation, or dance, or beatbox. I know it sounds funny, but it takes my mind off my nerves, and sometimes it also starts a good conversation. If I just act silly for a while I feel better!

Hang out with friends who make you feel good about yourself. Don't waste time on the 'popular' girls because they'll only make you feel inadequate—and for no reason. You have lots to give. Find your niche.

Set aside a day each week, free of study. Use this day to do whatever you want—just don't feel guilty! If you've worked hard enough through the week, you deserve this day off, so enjoy it while you can.

School doesn't have to be a fashion contest. It's okay to just wear the uniform. It's also okay to express yourself (without breaking uniform rules!) by making quirky additions to your school look.

Make a habit of checking your school diary every afternoon when you get home. You're much less likely to forget about homework if you get into the habit of using your diary regularly.

If you don't know what you want to do as a career, choose electives you enjoy. You'll do better at work you like, and it might point you towards a career you'd love to do but never considered.

If you really dislike your teacher, see if you can transfer to someone else's class. Be mature and give clear reasons why you wish to change. If your learning ability is being compromised, say so!

If you can't get the hang of a concept, try rephrasing it, drawing a diagram or making a flow chart or mind map. Often things make more sense when you're made to represent them visually or in another form.

Every school has bitches and bullies. If you're lucky you'll never have to come into contact with them. If you do find yourself in that situation, stand your ground and be assertive but not rude. Don't let them get to you! You're better than that.

Actively listening in class can help so much with learning. Try to really concentrate—rephrase key points in your head to drill them in. It helps with note-taking, too, because you'll know what you need to learn.

Make the most of school while you're there. Graduation comes about all too quickly and you might regret not taking opportunities you were offered. Doing as much as you can at school will also help you develop a killer resume. Take chances! It's worth it.

home life

Your house is your castle! It's important that you feel safe and happy at home. Sometimes siblings or your parents can get in the way of that, and it's helpful to know how to get around those little disagreements. Getting your room into shape helps wonders too.

You ...
and your parents

Parents and guardians are a bit of a minefield, really. If they're at all normal then you probably love them, and they love you too. Love is one thing. Getting along with them is another! However, once you work out a way to co-exist peacefully with your folks, life can be a lot easier. Try these ideas for making the most of your home life.

yourchores

We all know it—**chores suck.** Some days you'll come home from school and only want to watch TV. But unfortunately, helping out with the housework is necessary—and it's good practice for when you move out into your own home. Who's going to cook dinner when you live alone?

If there's a chore that you really hate doing, however, or if you have way too many chores and they're getting in the way of your study, **talk to your parents.** Try not to sound like you're accusing them of anything (for example, say 'I feel I have too many chores' instead of 'You've given me too many chores'), be calm, and try to keep the conversation light—make jokes, and be ready to negotiate. You might switch stacking the dishwasher with feeding the cat, for example. When you ask to have a chore removed from the list, explain exactly why, and again, be willing to bargain—you might end up with twice a week and you'll have to be happy with that.

yourrules

Every teenager has rules they have to live by—curfews, sleepover rules, bedtimes. Nine times out of ten, these rules are in place to **ensure your safety and wellbeing,** and it's easier just to follow them. However, occasionally your folks might not have thought a rule through and it'll put you in a difficult situation. For example, the play ends at 10pm. Mum says she can't pick you up after 9, so you say 'That's fine, I'll catch the train home with my friends.' Mum then says 'No, you know you're not allowed to catch the train home after dark'—so how the hell do you get home from the play?

Firstly, argue for the outcome you want most, but **be prepared to settle for less.** Maturely and calmly, tell your parent that all your friends who are going to the play with you will be catching the train home, and can you please know why aren't you allowed? If s/he is unwilling to bend on the train idea, say 'Okay, I'll need some money for a taxi, please, because that's the only other option I can think of'. Once she realises she's given you no other way to get home, she might agree to pick you up, or let you catch the train if you go with a friend. Breaking down rules like this is a lengthy process, so be patient and calm. Explain to your parents that you appreciate their concerns for your safety, but their rules shouldn't imprison you.

yourstories

Being able to **talk to your parents** can make life much more pleasant. If you don't feel like you have to lie to them, you'll often develop a much stronger bond through sharing issues with one another, and offering and receiving advice. But how do you get to that stage?

Say, 'I really want us to have an honest relationship. Am I allowed to talk to you about (my relationships/sex/parties/other awkward topic)?' Give them time to think about it. Chances are they'll understand your reasons and say they want to hear about it.

If they say they don't want to know, you might just need to accept that, but it's unlikely. The important thing is to be able to **laugh together.** Start with funny stories, and ease them into the idea that you're at this stage of life.

Eventually you'll build trust and openness, and you'll be able to share more embarrassing or shocking stories and ask for advice. Be as honest as you can when talking to your parents—they'll know when you're telling the truth and they'll appreciate it.

yourconnection

A lot of teenagers find themselves embarrassed by their parents. Society tells us it's not 'cool' to be seen out with our folks, and that we—for some reason—have to view them with disdain. This is a pretty shallow view of life. Your parents spent time, money and lots of energy raising you, and they want to be involved in seeing you grow up—into a teenager, and then into an adult. Most parents will give you space when you're a teenager because they know that you might be embarrassed of them. But life's so much better if you can get over that.

Try asking your parents out to lunch. Once you're at lunch, actually talk to your parents! They're not just parents, they're people—they have lives outside of taking care of you, and you might be surprised at what they've been up to lately. Don't be afraid to reciprocate—tell them what you think about school, what you want to do when you graduate, any of that. They'll be interested to hear about the directions you're taking in life.

Once you've done the lunch deal, try getting your mum or dad to take you shopping, out to coffee, or even out to an activity like seeing a movie or bowling. Parents can be so much fun

because they're a refreshing break from teenage conversation; they often have some hilarious views on the world.

If you take time like this, even just once a month, to catch up with your parents, you'll build a wonderful bond. **Daughters need their parents**—mothers can help you with girl issues, and you can build a bond with your father over common interests, such as movies. If you can actually share secrets with your folks, then you're very lucky—to have parents who are also your friends is a wonderful feeling!

SIBLINGS
... the best is yet to come

You hate your sister. Of course you do. You fight all the time and you think life would be easier if you were an only child. This is what life is like now, but it won't always be. Make the peace and you'll make a best friend for life.

The benefits of having a sister:

You can shop together.

You can borrow each other's clothes.

She'll be able to relate to you and give you advice when you complain about boys.

She can fix that annoying other hand where the nail polish always looks bad.

She'll keep your secrets ... most of the time!

She'll be honest with you about whether your outfit looks good or not.

You can have sleepovers ... without even leaving your house!

You'll have a best friend who lives metres away.

INVEST NOW, REAP BENEFITS LATER

Think of your relationship with your sibling as a fine wine. Right now, it's not so tasty, because it's new. What you need to do is take care of it, and give it a good few years. Then make the most of it when it tastes its best.

In other words, while your sister might be a total bully right now, if you play your cards right, she'll be someone you can rely on for the rest of your life. Just live out the fights and the stealing from each other's rooms, give as many second chances as you can bear to give, and wait and see what happens.

When you're both more mature, you'll suddenly realise that she's not so annoying anymore, and she'll think the same about you. Same goes for brothers. All of a sudden they'll be making jokes instead of just grunting in your general direction. Suddenly you'll have a friend who happens to live with you; someone you can trust, laugh with, and enjoy the company of. Truly, it happens! And it's really great when it does.

That being said, you can't force this development. It comes naturally when you're both a little older. For the time being, you can defuse situations with your siblings by proving to them that they can trust you. Try not to steal from their room, and be ready to forgive if they make a mistake that affects you. Stand up for yourself, but try not to distance them by being too harsh with your arguments. One day they'll realise that you're actually pretty awesome to live with, and the rest is all good.

For the time being, though, you need tools to get you through what's happening with your sibling right now, which might not be so much fun! Eventually you'll be adults who respect one another—and maybe even enjoy each other's company—but for the time being, communication is key.

Next time your older sibling steals something from your room, calmly ask for it back. When they return it, say 'Hey, next time, could you do me a favour and let me know you're taking this? I totally freaked out, I thought I'd lost it! Thanks, you're a legend!' You're not attacking them at all; you're asking for a favour, but you've avoided the fight, and they'll realise they've inconvenienced you.

If they have a go at you, it's probably because they feel guilty about doing something they know is wrong: stealing. Defuse the situation: instead of biting back, just say 'Hey, it's fine! I'm cool with you borrowing it, you know me though, I'm just so scatterbrained that I'll always assume I've lost it if I don't know you have it. It'd be really helpful if you wouldn't mind—even just leave me a note.'

If you really don't want that particular item borrowed, start by mentioning how expensive it was. 'Do you have my camera? It cost me $200, I'm going to be so mad if I lost it!' They might think twice next time if they know how much it set you back.

Siblings are like puppies for a while. You learn to play, to pick on each other and test each other's limits—but every now and then one of you will go too far. It can be a surprise when a joke your sister laughed at yesterday, she's suddenly yelling at you for today, but there are reasons for this and ways to fix things too!

Firstly, it helps to know why your sibling is suddenly mad at you. It doesn't take much: they might have had a bad day, or someone's said something to make them insecure and your joke or passing comment happens to tap into that. For example, if she's been at school where one of her friends made a joke about her curly hair, and when she comes home you make a similar joke—it might just be the final straw, but that's not your fault!

Don't take it personally if your sibling reacts irrationally. If they suddenly lash out at you for banter they would have laughed at yesterday, nothing works better than an honest 'Sorry, just kidding!' and a quick change of the subject. If it seems more serious than that, just try asking them what's wrong, and gently point out that you didn't mean to offend them. If they flare up, just apologise, keep your tone light, and change the subject.

If you've been finding yourself flaring up at your sibling lately, think about why. Are they making a

ben says "Ben has one little sister, and he lives with his two brothers. He says of his brothers, 'I get along really well with both of them now, but they don't get along with each other! They used to think they could pick on me because I'm the youngest, but they can't anymore'. Ben learnt how to earn his brothers' respect, and that's not impossible!"

repetitive joke that hits on your insecurities? Can you talk to them about it?

If a conversation about their joke will start with you baring your soul and ending with them laughing at you, your better option might just be to grit your teeth and bear it. After all, if it's just banter then they're not trying to hurt you, they're just playing. Take it how it's offered: as a joke.

Interpreting your sibling's words as a joke can often defuse a growing argument, as well. If your sibling is deliberately attempting to rile you up, try laughing at—and agreeing with—their insults. You don't have to believe them, just make them see that their words aren't hurting you! If they call you an idiot, just laugh and say 'Yeah, but you love me'. If they keep at it, keep your cool! You'll frustrate them more when they can't get you angry than you would if you flared up straight away.

The most important thing; just love your sibling the way they are. Love takes courage, but if you're brave enough to show your sibling, day by day, that you accept them, your friendship will bloom and you'll find yourselves in a really good place.

The benefits of having a brother:

You can impress boys with your sport knowledge, thanks to him.

You can borrow his games.

You can set him up with one of your friends—or vice versa!

He'll protect you if anybody hurts you.

He can frighten away boys that won't back off.

If you want to rearrange your room, just get him and his strong (hot!) friends to help.

He might never admit to thinking you were a good sister, but if anything ever happened, you know he'd be right there by your side.

What kind of sibling are you?

Are you a good sister? You might not think much of your siblings, but have you ever wondered what they think about you? You could ask them … or you could take this quiz and find out the easy (less soul-crushing!) way.

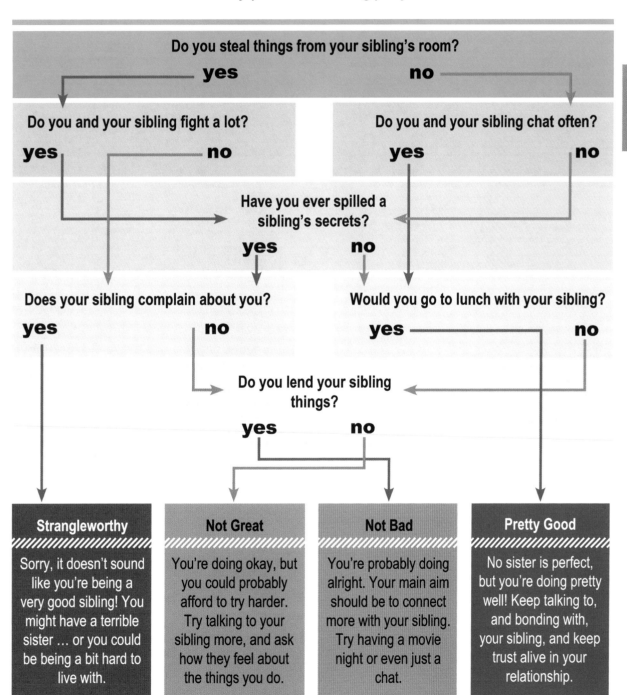

Do you steal things from your sibling's room?

yes — **no**

Do you and your sibling fight a lot?

yes — **no**

Do you and your sibling chat often?

yes — **no**

Have you ever spilled a sibling's secrets?

yes — **no**

Does your sibling complain about you?

yes — **no**

Would you go to lunch with your sibling?

yes — **no**

Do you lend your sibling things?

yes — **no**

Strangleworthy
Sorry, it doesn't sound like you're being a very good sibling! You might have a terrible sister … or you could be being a bit hard to live with.

Not Great
You're doing okay, but you could probably afford to try harder. Try talking to your sibling more, and ask how they feel about the things you do.

Not Bad
You're probably doing alright. Your main aim should be to connect more with your sibling. Try having a movie night or even just a chat.

Pretty Good
No sister is perfect, but you're doing pretty well! Keep talking to, and bonding with, your sibling, and keep trust alive in your relationship.

It's not what you say ...
IT'S THE WAY THAT YOU SAY IT

You might not hear the difference between 'I'll clean up later' and 'I will clean up, but in about an hour' but your parents will. Life at home can get tricky if you feel like your folks are always yelling at you, especially when it's somehow your fault but you don't know why. Try these simple tricks to improve communication at home and let your parents know you really DO mean to clean up!

The Problem

Adults hear differently to teenagers. I know it sounds ridiculous, but it's 100% true. What happens is that teenagers have their own way of communicating, which is—seriously, being honest—a slightly different language to the generation above. We use different words, tones, and even sentence structures. On top of that, adults are nearly always stressed or worried about something and likely to assume the worst, so when you say something that in YOUR language is a normal comment, they flip out because in THEIR language, it sounds like an insult!

It sounds impossible, but all you have to do is learn to speak their language. Partly this will mean you

communicate more clearly, and partly this involves employing calm language that doesn't come off as aggressive. The minute an adult thinks they hear aggression—even when you really didn't mean it that way—they get defensive, and we all know that's not worth the hassle.

Luckily, it's easy to defuse the situation. You just have to think in advance about what you're going to say and how best to get the response you want, whether it's a 'Yes, you can go to the party' or 'No, that's fine, I'll stack the dishwasher in a minute'. All communication is manipulation—we all want something, which is why we speak—so here's how to get that working for you!

THE SCENARIO: You're in the kitchen, Mum's doing her hair, you have five minutes till you need to leave for the school bus and she hasn't made your lunch yet. You're happy to do it for yourself, but you need to make sure first that she hasn't made it.

YOU (would normally) SAY: 'Have you done the lunches yet, or do I have to do them?'

SHE HEARS: 'I expect you to do the lunches every single day, and I don't want to help you, so hurry up and finish the lunches—I don't care what your hair looks like or that you're stressed, I just want my food.' She'll naturally respond by yelling at you or getting stressed—wouldn't you?

SAY INSTEAD: 'Can I do the lunches, or have you done them already?'
Saying it this way not only expresses ('Can I') that you're happy to do the lunches, but the use of the word 'already' will make it clear to her that you realise she usually always does them on time.

THE SCENARIO: You need a lift to a friend's and you know it'll be inconvenient for your Dad to drive you. He's tired when he gets home from work but you can't go to your mate's earlier than 7pm.

YOU (would normally) SAY at 6:45pm: 'Can I have a lift to Ellen's at 7?'

HE HEARS: 'I don't care that you're exhausted, I want to go to my friend's place and it's your responsibility to take me.' If he's really stressed he might also assume that you don't want to be at home with him, and then a whole mess of argument comes up as to why not.

SAY INSTEAD as early as possible!: 'I'm really sorry to ask this because I know you're tired, but I need a lift to Ellen's. I can't get a lift with anyone else—could you please take me? Whenever's good for you is fine, I just can't go before 7pm.'
Acknowledging that he's been to work and is tired is a great way to bring down anybody's defences. He'll also appreciate that you tried elsewhere (even if by 'tried' you texted one friend and said 'Can I have a lift, it's cool if not'!) and will be more willing to make the effort if you're flexible. You might end up going at 7:30 so he can watch his favourite TV show, but it's worth it for the fight-free lift, right?

Words to Avoid

ALWAYS/NEVER: You say 'I never ask you for anything,' which prompts your parent to list all the times that you do! They'll pounce on words like 'always' and 'never' so try not to be too absolute.

HAVE TO: 'I have to go to my friend's place,' 'Do I have to do the dishes?'—try saying instead 'I'd really like to go to my friend's place' and 'Am I on dish duty tonight?' 'Have to' implies force and when it comes to chores, it'll give the idea that it's something you don't want to do. (Which might be true, but they don't have to know that!)

LATER: 'I'll do it later' is the universal code for 'It's never going to happen'. If s/he says 'Clean the table', reply instead with 'I'm just about to—can I do it in about five minutes?' It will make the parent feel they've been heard, and a specific time frame will mean they're more likely to believe you mean what you say, and drop it.

Words to Use

No adult can turn down a 'please,' 'if you wouldn't mind,' 'if it's not a problem,' 'I'm happy to do that for you,' 'you're welcome,' 'I understand,' and the classic 'thank you'—don't forget the angelic smile!

Independence:
EARN IT AND KEEP IT

You're just itching for the day when you can drive, live alone and make your own rules, aren't you? Good news: you can still be independent (to an extent!) while living with your family. It's all about flexibility and knowing your limits!

WHAT IS INDEPENDENCE?

Independence is much more than being able to stay out all night without being grounded. It's about taking responsibility for yourself; knowing what's right, knowing what's good for you, and knowing when to say no. An independent person has enough life experience to make their own decisions, and enough strength to accept and deal with the consequences when their decisions go wrong!

It's the kind of thing that comes naturally as you get older; more and more you'll be learning life lessons in your interactions with friends and at work. As you get older you'll probably learn to drive, you'll go out more and to different places (less sleepovers, more

night clubs!), and you'll be making your own plans without relying on your parents to get you from A to B. This is all part of learning who you are, trusting yourself and being a young adult.

A huge part of gaining independence is—you guessed it—earning it from your parents. Like it or not, parents and guardians play a huge role in how self-reliant you are, or are allowed to be. If you're never allowed out, independence in terms of social outings will be harder to gain, but by the same token, if you're allowed out all the time and you never have to do any chores, independence in terms of managing responsibility is something you won't have learnt yet!

True independence comes when your parents don't have to be your parents; they become your roommates. This happens when you're cleaning and cooking without them asking you, and they're happy for you to make your own plans and make your own way from place to place. It's a balance of power, a trade-off; you ease their burden of parenting and they help you become an adult!

ARE YOU GAINING INDEPENDENCE?

You know you're becoming independent when ...
- you can cook yourself dinner
- you know the difference between detergent powder and washing powder!
- you're paying for your own clothes from the money you earn in your after-school job
- you can tell your parents what your plans are for the weekend, without having to ask permission for every single one
- you know which night is bin night
- you study, clean and go to bed without having to be asked or ordered into it
- you have your own key to the house
- you make appointments and phone calls to places like the bank—your parents don't have to do it for you
- you can say 'I'm just off to Anna's for the afternoon', hop in your car, and drive away
- you catch yourself making a budget ...
- you respect your parents for who they are, instead of being caught up on the idea that they're only there to ruin your life!

THE UPS AND DOWNS OF INDEPENDENCE

YOU'LL NEED TO:

Learn not to blame your parents when things go wrong for you.

Draw the line between independence and selfishness; sometimes you need to put family, work or school before your own plans and that's part of being an adult.

Take the cons of independence with the pros—keep your room clean, help with chores—a roommate would do that, so why not a daughter?

Keep safe! True independent adults know how to take care of themselves, especially when out at night. Know the risks and learn how to minimise them.

YOU GET TO:

Make your own decisions on where you want to be and when.

Feel good about the fact that your parents trust you to make your own decisions.

Run your own daily schedule: you study, sleep, and get yourself ready for school when you want and how you want.

Ask for help when you need it; if you're not having your parents make your decisions all the time, when you do need help to decide something, they'll be more likely to assist you.

Get a taste of adult life without the financial stress!

get cashed up:

HAVE A LIFE WITH NEXT TO NOTHING

So, you make about $10 a week, and that's only when you get around to doing the ironing. It vanishes pretty quickly, doesn't it? Try these money-safe tips to make it last.

SAVE YOUR CHANGE - EVERY CENT

Every time you break a note, take home the change and put it in a piggy bank. No, you don't need a porcelain pig: a gift bag or empty chocolate box serves the same purpose and doesn't set you back twenty bucks!

Put every coin you receive into the box, and then when you go out, only take out what you need for train fare, etc. This will keep you from spending just to get rid of your shrapnel, and it'll start adding up before you know it.

THE MAGIC WORD - BUDGET

It sucks, and you'll need a calculator, but it helps so much. Sit down and work out how much you make a week. Add in your job if you have one, pocket money, and an estimate of odd job money if your funds work that way.

From that total, take out what you spend each week on the school canteen, train fares, movies, and so on. This not only lets you know how much you should have left, but it also gives you a good idea of where your money is going, and where you can afford to cut back.

If you spend $7 a week on sausage rolls at school,

find an alternative that you can make at home and save yourself that money for socialising.

If, at the end of the week, you've met your budget with money left over, be smart! Save it. Put it aside, in a piggy bank or bank account; do that every week that you reach Sunday with cash to spare, and that way, on really social, busy weeks, you'll have that extra cash to keep you going.

BANK ACCOUNTS - TOO EASY

Open an account with your local bank. Start with a normal account, and get into the habit of making deposits. If your work pays you online, give them the details to your account.

The main benefit of debit card over cash is that you aren't so conscious of how much you have: it'll add up quickly if you don't touch your account for a week or two. Be careful when spending with your card, though: when you're not actually handing over cash it might feel like you're not spending at all. Avoid the shopping hangover and know exactly how much you have on the card before you use it!

If you're making a little more and you're saving for something like a new bike or a gap year holiday, open a high-interest savings accounts. Most banks have accounts that reward you when you make regular deposits and never take cash out, so attach this account to your main one, but don't get a card for it—avoid temptation. If the only way you can access your account is through internet banking, you're less likely to dip into your savings, and more likely to ring up all that bonus interest!

Make sure you don't get overenthusiastic with your deposits, though: you can always make a second deposit if you have more to put in—it's better than putting too much in and sacrificing that interest in order to withdraw cash!

THINK BEFORE YOU SPEND

You have a bottle of water in your bag, so don't buy juice at the canteen! That $3 could be put towards a new dress this summer. Think how much a little saving will get you, and put your wallet back in your pocket.

Keeping a savings diary is a good way to cut your spending habits. If you're forced to admit, on paper—or even on a blog where people can judge!—that you wasted $20 on a shoddy craft set and now you can't afford that pro easel until July, you'll be much less likely to splurge in the first place. Be vigilant with your diary and soon you'll find your daily totals are dropping.

A NEW KIND OF GENEROSITY

Don't go out and buy your best friend a $50 body lotion set. Chances are she already has stacks of products just like that 'unique' bath soak, and she'll be your best friend whether you spend $50 or $5 on her, so get creative instead. Buy her a small gift, and make the main gift truly unique.

gorgeous cake. If you have a little more money to spend, get some photos printed (you can get them printed cheaply at chain stores and online) and make her a photo album, scrapbook or collage frame. It'll be such a thoughtful, unique and personal gift that she'll feel like it's worth a million bucks!

If you're not at all crafty, then write her a poem (a hilarious one always goes down well), or even buy her an affordable item of jewellery and hide the box inside a tin of her favourite lollies. And no gift is better for a bestie than that $2 birthday tiara or sash that she has to wear all day!

KNOWING WHEN TO SPLURGE

If you're careful with money when you need to be, when it comes to that extra special occasion such as your Dad's 50th or that fancy dinner out, you'll be able to buy a nice gift and a new dress without hating yourself for it.

It's okay to spoil yourself occasionally—if you've just finished an insanely hard exam and all you can think about is chocolate, treat yourself. Money is there to make your life easier, and you should be able to spend it how you like—but it's all about moderation! Save a little, spend a little. Strike a balance between being be too stingy and splashing out too often.

With a little bit of foresight (you'll clearly need money in March because your Mum and brother both have birthdays, so start cutting corners in February) and following your money rules carefully, you'll find you can afford to be generous when it really counts, and you'll have the cash to enjoy yourself. And what's more enjoyable—that one CD, or dinner and the movies with all your friends? Your call!

You still want a life, even when you don't have money. The good news is—you can have both! Just try these ideas for cash-free socialising.

SKIP THE ENTRY FEE

Instead of ice skating and the movies, try a place without a fee attached:

- picnic in the park
- window shopping (be strong!)
- a day in the city (walk to save cash)
- movie night at someone's house
- sleepovers
- bushwalks and sightseeing
- lunch out (go somewhere cheap!)
- spend the day with your friends making each other up and taking photos
- hold a clothes and accessories swap party. Everyone comes over for a night, or for the afternoon, and brings all their clothes and accessories they're bored with—and then you swap! Free clothes, no fee, and you get rid of your old stuff.

CUT CORNERS WHERE IT COUNTS

You can still have a glamorous day out if you know where to save the money!

Say you're visiting an art gallery during the day, then going out to dinner. You need nice clothes, entry fee, dinner money, transport; those are a given. But you can still do the day for less!

- Borrow your dinner dress from a friend. It won't cost you a cent and you'll still have that 'new dress' feel.
- Bring your own lunch to the gallery. Cafeteria prices just aren't worth it!
- If you each pay for only what you buy at dinner, you can save money by drinking water and skipping dessert (and it's better for you, too!)
- See if you can get a lift to or from each event. Or if the train is cheaper than the bus, you know what to do. Better yet, can you walk? Get some incidental exercise, and save the money!

'Borrow a dress from a friend. It won't cost you a cent and you'll still have that "new dress" feel.'

PLAN AHEAD AND STICK TO IT

So, you've been invited to the biggest party of the year. You really want to go, and you want to look great.

You can do all that and still have a life now! Time to start the party fund.

- First, work out how long you have until the party, and how much money you'll need (a dress could be $40, then $60 for shoes?)
- Use a box, money box or envelope especially for your party fund; it'll make it easier to see just how much you have, and the special box or envelope will keep you from being tempted to spend it on other things.
- Then, start saving! Cut corners where you can, and put any extra cash you have aside towards the fund.
- Don't put too much each week into the fund and cut yourself short: you don't want to be broke and dipping into the fund, because if you get into that habit the money will vanish fast!
- When you do have the money, relax, go shopping and enjoy yourself! If you spend it all, that's fine—that's what you've saved it up for. And if you have cash left over, all the better! Saving can only end well.

million dollar models

WHAT WOULD YOU DO WITH A MILLION DOLLARS?

We asked our models; 'If you had a million dollars and only one day to spend it, what would you do with it?' Read on for the answers ... whether you donate to charity or not, spending a million dollars would still be a huge help for your country's economy!

Buy a house in Tuscany, and gorgeous Italian furniture to go in it.
                                        - Harriet

I'd give half to charity, a quarter for buying presents for family and friends and a quarter for me to spend however I want!
                                        - Anna

A car, a few investment properties, and clothes ...
                                        - Kelli

Give most away to charity, then go clothes shopping. Also, I'd buy a cool camera.
                                        - Georgia A

Buy HEAPS of clothes :D
                                        - Chané

I would buy a few nice things for myself ... and give the rest to my sponsor child in Senegal for her to have a chance in a good career and education.
                                        - Caroline

Buy lots of shoes :)
                                        - Cara

I would go on a holiday with all of my friends and buy them presents.
                                        - Blake

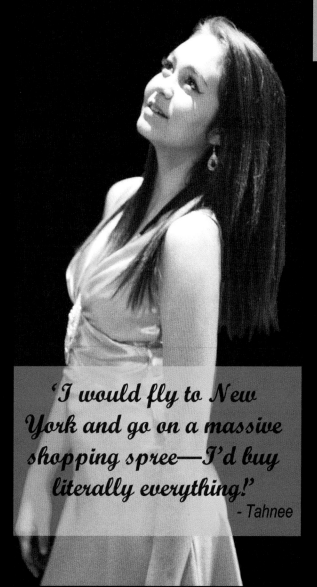

'I would fly to New York and go on a massive shopping spree—I'd buy literally everything!'
                                        - Tahnee

YOUR HAVEN: *Your Room*

Your room is where you'll chill out, sleep, entertain friends, avoid the world, and study throughout high school. It can become completely dedicated to schoolwork, or you can make it your study-free haven. It's up to you. Most students go somewhere in between—here's how to strike a balance.

yourbed

You'll be needing lots of sleep in high school, so make sure your bed is comfortable! Invest in nice pillows and try to keep it made—your bed should be only for bedding, but never for school folders or your bag.

If you're having trouble sleeping because school thoughts are invading your mind, try the following tips:

- Don't study in bed. Your brain needs to associate bed with sleep, not learning!
- Don't have much sugar within the last three hours before going to bed.
- Develop a wind-down ritual—take a bath and iron your clothes for the next day. Don't do anything too energetic before bed.
- If you've studied enough during the day, you don't need to think of school at night. Tell your brain you've learnt enough and now's time for sleeping. Weirdly, that works.
- Try spending the last hour of the day in low lighting. Your brain associates bright lights with sunlight and tries to keep you awake. Turn a lamp on to help your brain realise it's night!

yourdesk

Organisation is really important here. Clear out your desk completely and start again. If you have a computer, install that first, because that has to be placed well so you don't get uncomfortable working at it (that's called ergonomics, by the way). Then organise your books and folders around it. It helps to have a diary that you can lay flat on the desk to record assignment due dates and so on, and of course, a pen! Invest in some stacked in-trays that you can use to keep notes to be filed in, or homework to be done.

Some students buy a binder folder for each subject—make sure you invest in a hole-punch, and keep the binders somewhere easily accessible—they'll get heavy towards the end of semester and you don't want to do your back in trying to lift one up from the floor! Make sure all your study tools—folders, hole-punch, highlighters, diary, computer—are within arm's reach of your desk chair.

yourwall

If you have even a square inch of space on your bedroom wall, fill it with school stuff. One way is to invest in a whiteboard and a corkboard. On the whiteboard you can write important dates and reminders—or a countdown to graduation!—and on the corkboard you can pin up assignment sheets, forms, stuff you need to remember, etc. If there's something in a subject that you just can't get into your head, print it and stick it to your wall. If you're seeing it every day, you're more likely to absorb it.

yourbookcase

If you haven't got much room on your desk, your bookcase can come in handy. Bookcases don't necessarily have to be just for books—you can even put a mirror at the back of one shelf and have a cosmetics/hair styling section, toys and trinkets on another shelf, and save the rest for books and magazines. If you're using your bookcase to store school stuff as well as regular books, make sure you separate the two. Use an easily accessible shelf for your school stuff—your regular books are less likely to be accessed in these years and so can go on a higher or lower shelf.

Your bedside table can actually be really useful in staying sane at high school. Your must-haves include a lamp, a stereo alarm—one that you can set your own music to, like an iPod stereo—a small notepad, a pen, a book you enjoy reading, your phone and phone charger, your hairbrush, and then any essentials you use all the time like deodorant or mascara. If all your must-haves are on the one table, you can be half ready for school by the time you get out of bed!

As for the iPod stereo—this little trick is an awesome way to get you out of bed in the mornings. Before you go to bed at night, choose a song that really motivates you. It doesn't have to have motivating lyrics, it might just be that the beat makes you want to dance or the song makes you think of the gap year holiday you've been planning. Set your alarm to wake you up with that song. When you do wake up, don't hit 'snooze'—let the song play out. You'll feel much more willing to bounce out of bed and

get ready while dancing to it, than you'd feel if you woke up to that incessant 'beep-beep-beep' of most alarms. Keep the music playing while you get ready. You'll have much more energy, get ready faster and you're likely to concentrate better in your first lessons of the day, because you're actually awake for once!

Another alarm tip for extreme weather—employ the gorgeous, wonderful snooze button. When your alarm wakes you up in winter, the last thing you want to do is get up from your beautiful, warm bed, to brave the cold while getting changed for school. So, if you have a heater in your room—set your alarm ten minutes early, and when it goes off, hit snooze, turn the heater on and go back to sleep for ten minutes. Then when you actually need to get out of bed, the chill will be out of the air and you can get dressed near the heater, making it much more bearable. Same goes for summer—wake up the air-con before you do!

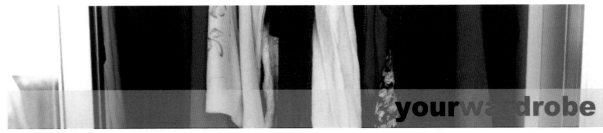

If you organise your wardrobe well enough, you can basically crawl out of bed and dress for school without even opening your eyes. Hang all your clothes however you want, but if, within each section, you put all your school clothes to the left (or right), it makes it much easier to find them when the sun's hardly up and you're practically still asleep!

It also helps to put your school clothes in sections. You could even hang all your singlets on the one hanger, then all your blouses together, and so on. If you have, for example, a vest that you always wear with the same shirt, why not hang them up together? And keep your school shoes easily accessible. Nothing sucks more than missing the bus because you can't find your joggers!

... home alone?

It's dead scary being home on your own. You might be fine during the day, but once night falls, nobody can deny that your every second thought is about zombies and burglars! Try these tips to get through the night.

Lights and music will keep your mind from going too crazy. Keep your iPod playing or the TV on, and leave a light on in the centre of your house, or near the front and back doors. Sleep in the light if you need to!

Get defensive! Think, 'This is MY home. Nobody is allowed in MY home without my knowledge or permission.' Get your anger to overtake your fear. And keep that heavy textbook handy to knock that burglar out with.

Make it obvious that someone's home. Every now and then, turn on and off lights in a walking pattern through the house. Keep the outside light on if you need to.

Make sure you know how long you'll be alone for. If you think your sister's coming home at 11pm and she opens the door at 8pm, you'll freak right out.

If you have a dog, relax! Dogs will bark long before you hear even a footstep. And a dog is a very good defence against zombies. Also, zombies aren't real. Just in case that slipped your mind.

Distract yourself. Watch TV, read a book, exercise. When you eventually go to bed, try to think about what you just saw or read, as opposed to focusing on your fears. Failing that, just concentrate on breathing in, out, in, out ... you'll be asleep in no time.

If you get really afraid, call or text a friend or go on Facebook. Find some conversation to distract you. You might even have that friend down the street who can come up for a few hours. Failing that, at least distract yourself chatting until you can't keep your eyes open!

What you deserve AT HOME

Your Rights

You have the right to:

- feel safe at home. If you're scared to come home for reasons of abuse of any kind, drug use or other dangerous situation, talk to an adult or teacher, or call a help service (such as the Kids Helpline in Australia).
- trust your family. If you can't, try to find people you can trust, like uncles and aunts or the parents of your friends.
- your own space and sense of privacy. If your little brother has worked out how to pick your lock and you can't even study alone, let alone have friends or boyfriends over, speak to your parents about your right to a space that's yours and yours alone.
- fair use of the house. If you can't make lunch for school because your Dad watches TV in the kitchen, it may be time to have a chat.

Your Responsibilities

You have the responsibility to:

- do your chores when you're asked to do them.
- be respectful when using someone else's property. Think how you'd feel if your Mum watched TV in your bed—without asking—and left a slice of half-eaten pizza on your bedside table, and crumbs everywhere. You'd flip, wouldn't you? So don't be surprised if she freaks out, too.
- communicate with your family. If you can't remember the last time you did anything but grunt in their general direction, it's time to acknowledge that they're human, and maybe have a chat. Or at least try to answer them with more than a few words!
- ensure that home is a safe place for the rest of your family too. If your sibling barely comes home because the two of you fight so much, think about how you can change that.
- help out when needed! You're all people, and a day in the garden with Grandpa can actually be really enjoyable.

ten toptips about home

Your room is your haven. Take care of it. Make it your place to be away from the world, to study in peace, to chill out when you need to relax. Keep it clean and organised and it'll be your little sanctuary.

When negotiating with parents, try to stay good-humoured. Be assertive, but try never to get angry or raise your voice—sudden anger will only make them surer of their decision, and they'll view you as immature.

Remember that your younger siblings are probably only bugging you because they enjoy your company, or want your approval. It can get frustrating, but it's important to remember that it's done with love!

Home should be a place you want to come to. If your siblings or parents are making home a stressful place, or a place you'd rather avoid, you need to speak to somebody about it, like a counsellor or help service.

Planning your time effectively not only means you'll get study and exercise done, you'll also have time to chill out and read or watch TV, guilt-free. Think about that next time you're on Facebook in study time!

A corkboard and whiteboard in your room are so vital to getting organised. Pin your assignments up on the corkboard, write deadlines on the whiteboard—you can suddenly be that awesome friend who remembers birthdays, too.

Talk to your parents when you're entering senior years. Explain to them that you might be stressed. Insist that you want to get along well with them, and be clear about ways in which they can help you.

When you need to talk to your parents about something awkward, often having notes can help you. It feels weird to read off the page, but it'll help you get the message across with more clarity.

Investing in a good relationship with your parents and siblings can make life during high school so much easier. If getting along well with them means doing chores or coming home before midnight, maybe it's worth the sacrifices.

Once you get older, you'll have opportunities to develop a really good relationship with your siblings. Sisters can share clothes and go shopping, or you could ask for your brother's approval of your boyfriend.

social life

This is the fun part. Keep your friends beside you and high school will be a breeze. But balancing friends and school can be a little tricky, and alcohol in the equation sometimes doesn't help. Here's how to be a good friend while still having a great time out.

Social Networking: THE RULES

No matter what the website, the same rules apply. With the right approach, you can have a popular profile, catch up with your friends, and have a lot of fun. Break the rules, though, and things might get a little out of hand.

Maturity is the main thing you need to embody on social networks. If you bear in mind that everyone has the right to their own opinions, and try to keep your comments positive or at least constructive (and intelligent!) in their criticism, then you'll do fine. Put up photos of yourself with friends rather than photos of you in your bathroom in a bikini. Girls can get bitchy, especially with the protection of a computer, and you don't want to find yourself labelled a 'slut' because of some photos. For the same reason, watch what you say to other people's boyfriends! Unfortunately, some teenagers think it's cool to be offended, so you'll occasionally get into a tiff no matter what you do. Just remember to follow the **ten golden rules** of social networking, and you can minimise the amount of times this happens!

1. Don't lie about your age! Even if you think you look it. It's easy math to tell you're lying, and you'll look like a loser.

2. You don't need to post bulletins advertising your new photo. People will comment it if they want to.

3. That photo of you in your bikini, pouting, then tinted to make you look tanned? Not as attractive as you might think.

4. That photo of you laughing away with your friends, dressed like an idiot? A *lot* more attractive than you might think!

5. DON'T get too brave on your keyboard! If you wouldn't say it face-to-face, don't say it in cyber-space. Be nice.

6. Don't be rude, or make it personal, when debating over bands and celebrities. They wouldn't get bitchy for you.

7. Don't put any phone numbers or addresses online. You never know who might be looking, and you never know what they might do. Just play it safe.

8. Don't put slutty photos up. It might seem like fun now, but when you're going for a job in two years' time …

9. Positive comments are so much more fun than negative ones. You'll instantly be more popular online.

10. It's supposed to be fun! Enjoy yourself. Don't let rude people put you down—keep being yourself.

I'll be there for you ...

In all the TV shows, best friends know exactly how to act. She—or he, but for now let's just say she—knows how your brain works, you know you can make jokes without offending her, and when one of you is upset, the other comes to the rescue. It'd be great if life was like that, but unfortunately, we're human! But you can try. Follow these simple rules to be a great best friend.

1 Don't expect your friend to be perfect. She might be awesome, but she's human, and we all make mistakes. Before you write her off completely for borrowing a pen from a girl you hate, think how you'd feel if she did that to you. A forgiving friend is a good friend!

2 **Try to know and remember what's important to your friend: her birthday, favourite colour, dream job, and the traits that she values, like honesty, loyalty or respect.**

3 Don't be afraid to stand up for yourself! It's okay to disagree with your bestie, especially when it's little things like your favourite band or celebrity. Be yourself around your friends; you don't need to suck up to them and say what you think they want to hear— you're entitled to your own opinion!

4 It's okay to occasionally rely on your friend. If you're having a terrible day, or you really need some advice, call her! Your best friend should be someone you can trust with your secrets, and who won't judge you too harshly when you do something silly. So if you have a problem, ask your bestie for advice! She'll be pleased to feel needed and to know you value her opinions. Try to be understanding and trustworthy when she's the one in need of advice, too.

Keep your in-jokes sacred. If you had a hilarious incident at a sushi bar once, and it's been a while since you saw your bestie, text her about it—even just 'hey! @ the sushi bar where you choked on that salmon roll ... the manager is staring at me, i think he remembers!' You'll give her a laugh and strengthen your bond. Don't bring up in-jokes too frequently, though, or they'll eventually stop being funny, and that's a shame!

5

6 Value your friend, but try not to be possessive. If your bestie feels like she can't ever hang out with anyone else without you being there, she may start to resent you. You don't have to spend every weekend together, and it's healthy to have other friends too! She's still your BFF.

Your bestie is the perfect person to try something new with. Terrified of rollercoasters? Enlist her to force you onto one with her. New experiences are always less scary when you're with a friend!

7

8 Help keep your friend out of trouble. This may mean you being the bad guy: if she wants to do something really dangerous like taking drugs from a stranger, or something you know she'll regret like hooking up with that guy, be the voice of reason. You can't force her into doing or not doing something, but you can help her understand she has choices. If she goes ahead and does it anyway, be clear that you told her not to, but don't make her feel worse than she already might—leave her to fix her own mistakes once she knows your opinion.

top **tip** - being supportive

If your friend's gone through something pretty tough, it's your duty as a BFF to help her through it. Here are some ways to help without overstepping your boundaries:

- Never compare her experience to your own. If she's just lost her grandfather, don't tell her how much 'worse' it was when you lost yours.
- Don't say 'relax', 'chill out' or 'it'll be fine'. It might sound like you're dismissing her problem or telling her she's being dramatic.
- Ask her if she wants to talk to you about it. If she hits you with a 'you wouldn't understand', don't beg. Just say 'Well, I'm here if you need me,' and leave it at that. She'll discuss it if she wants to.
- If she speaks to you about it, listen quietly. Empathise, but positively—say 'You're so strong' instead of 'You must feel awful'. Reminding someone of their own strength and capability is much more supportive than making them feel isolated by their experience.

PLAYING WITH FIRE: WHY GOSSIP IS RISKY

You were having a great time discussing those horrible shoes your mutual friend wore, until you get a text that makes your heart race: 'Belinda told me she heard you laughing about my shoes. You know I can't afford nice stuff right now, why would you say that?' Yep—now you're the bitch, and it seemed harmless at the time, right?

Gossip never seems hurtful while you're laughing with your friends. You might think you're making a little joke about that girl's annoying habit of saying 'well, duh!' but the next time she's talking to you and you all break out laughing when she says it, she's going to cotton on pretty quickly.

The thing about gossip—other than the fact that it hurts the person you're laughing about—is that if people know you're open to gossiping about others, they'll naturally feel quite comfortable about laughing at you. It's the same with keeping secrets: if you're always telling everyone else's secrets then people will assume you don't care about your own privacy either. They won't even realise you'd be offended if they gossiped or shared your secrets.

The other negative outcome is that people won't trust you. The more you spill secrets and bitch about others, the less people will tell you about themselves—they might still like you as a person but they'll trust you less and less.

BREAKING THE CYCLE

Follow these tips to eliminate gossip for good:

- When the gossip is about you, call them out on it immediately. Say 'I heard that you said this—do you have a problem with me or something?' Do it face-to-face so they can't ignore you or back out. Once they apologise, leave it be; it's not worth dragging out the fight.
- The next time you go to gossip about someone else, think how you'd feel if they found out—and think how you'd feel if they were saying these things about you.
- If you want to stop your friends gossiping, say 'Aw, I think her shoes are cute' or 'Come on, we all have stupid things we say too often!' to bring them back to reality. Don't be self-righteous about it, especially if you used to gossip too—just gently remind them that they probably shouldn't be saying these things.

Beauty:
why are we so obsessed?

From catwalk models to magazine covers, and even your friends on a day-to-day basis, perceptions of beauty, health and the 'right' way to look are everywhere. Why do we care so much about what we look like? And how do we keep it from affecting our lives?

Beauty is in the eye of the beholder. It's a quote we've all heard a million times, and it has a million different applications to life. It means beauty is subjective. It means what you find beautiful, your friend might hate. It means you might see something nobody else sees. It means that we cannot set or compare standards of attractiveness. And yet we do! Why is it that we judge ourselves and compare ourselves to others, with full knowledge that beauty doesn't work that way?

Unfortunately, that dilemma is a question without an answer. Despite continually being told not to compare ourselves to celebrities, teenage girls just can't help it. We've been brought up in a world of billboards, Photoshop and plastic surgery, and that's nobody's fault. We're in a world now, where beauty can be bought, and yet it remains as elusive as ever.

If the way you look is a constant source of stress and worry for you, you're one of the millions of teenage girls whose perceptions of beauty have been warped by the media. You're not seeing yourself clearly when you look in the mirror; instead of seeing yourself, just as you are, you're seeing a database of flaws and your brain is automatically running through that cherished list of celebrities you'd love to look like. Exhausting, isn't it?

And here's the silly part—we're quite literally comparing apples and pears. Here you are, a teenage girl who does her own makeup—and you probably do a damn good job at it too. But you're on a budget, you go to school and that last picture of you was taken on your friend's dodgy old phone— so why, why, why are you comparing yourself to an adult woman with her own personal makeup artist and hairdresser, who has had ten thousand dollars worth of plastic surgery, been professionally photographed in a well-lit studio, and then had that image edited? How is that anything like what you are? If you were that celebrity, you'd know for sure that this type of beauty is a lie. An illusion. It's a high-tech magic trick. These women go home to their partners, take off their makeup and wash their hair, and that night, they look completely normal. We just never see that side of them.

The good news is—despite the fact that the world is obsessed with beauty, you don't have to be. It's not an overnight process but you can train your brain to accept the way you look, and most importantly, to stop comparing you to adult women who are only ever photographed with high quality cameras.

The first way to start accepting your own brand of beauty is to see it. Look in the mirror, but this time, really look. What do you like about yourself? Are your wrists nice and slender? Do you have a cute ski-jump nose? Are your eyes a nice colour? You could even have amazing curly hair. You just probably never noticed these things because you were focusing on that one crooked tooth or measuring your ears.

Even more importantly, value what's inside. You may not have the lips and eyes of a celebrity, but you could have the brain of a genius or the heart of a lion! You could be healthy, hilarious, or loyal. Those are more important than what you look like any day. Do you pick your friends based on their lip-to-eye ratio? Of course not! (And if you do, you might need to sort that out!) Most likely you value their sense of humour, approach to learning or even the fact that they support the same football team as you. When you really think about it, what does the way we look have to do with anything? And when we're all so different inside, why is it surprising that we're different on the outside too?

Give yourself a break. You don't need to be stick thin or blonde to be gorgeous. You're beautiful because you're a good person, and that's the kind of beauty that counts.

five sticky situations

... and how to get through them, dignity intact!

You show up to a party as a zombie ... and nobody else is in costume

First, take several deep breaths and try not to cry. Then put your game face on. The bitch who told you it was a costume party is about to get her own back: whenever anyone asks what the deal is, tell them. Say it casually so it's not like you're bitching; 'Oh, Alana told me it was a costume party! I guess it was a joke, but I fell for it!'. Then, be the life of the party! Take photos with people, dance in character—show her that her cruel joke doesn't affect you.

You just farted loudly ... in the middle of a speech to your whole class

Things like this can be absolutely mortifying, but you have two options. You can cry and storm out of the room and have people laugh about it behind your back for months, or you can stay there, make a joke, laugh about it, and have the story die down within a few days. If you can laugh at yourself, it will limit the gossip, and when people see you're not being sensitive about it, they'll admire you.

You accidentally spilled your best friend's secret ... to her worst enemy

Damage control is important here! Make sure said enemy knows she absolutely mustn't tell anyone the secret. Then keep a close eye on her. Ask a friend to report back to you if she hears the gossip, if possible. Whether or not you tell your best friend your mistake is up to you—if you do tell her, be prepared for anger and be prepared to be humble about it. She may get revenge by spilling a secret of yours. Just try your hardest to keep the secret from spreading.

You were making jokes about a friend ... who was standing right behind you at the time

If you really can't stand this girl, this could be your way out of the friendship, but be prepared to have a possible enemy. Otherwise, apologise immediately. Take her away from the group and say 'I'm sorry, I shouldn't have said those things, I don't mean them at all. I was just being stupid. I understand if it takes you a while, but I hope you can forgive me.' She may be gracious, or she may ignore you for a few days; don't bring it up again unless she does, and just wait it out.

You ditched a friend to go to a party instead ... and she found out

Honesty is the best policy here. Was there a guy you liked at the party? And why didn't you just take your friend to the party too, instead of bailing on her? Just explain exactly what happened, apologise, and leave it at that. Give her space, and don't pressure her to forgive you. She's within her rights to be mad. Be honest, say sorry, and see how things go.

JUST SAY NO

It's easy to say to yourself 'I don't drink,' 'I don't want to try drugs' or 'I'm not ready to have sex'. You might wholeheartedly believe that—but getting someone else to back off is a whole different story. Have trouble getting your friends to take no for an answer? Read this.

Be Consistent

If sometimes you smoke and sometimes you don't, it's going to be a lot harder to get your friends to back off when they're offering you a cigarette and you're not keen. Set your rules. It doesn't mean that you have to smoke all the time if you say you smoke, but it makes it easier to turn people down if you never smoke—and stick to that rule.

Be Assertive

There's nothing like a calm smile and a killer line. Have reasons why you don't want whatever is being offered to you, but don't pull the reasons out until you have to. For example:

HER Do you want a cigarette?

YOU No thanks, I don't smoke.

HER Come on, have one.

YOU Nah, not interested, thanks!

HER Why not? We're all smoking.

YOU Yeah, after watching my grandfather smoke himself to death, I'm really not into going down the same path, thanks.

Your reason will most likely shock her into submission (use a real reason, don't lie!). It's more effective to just say no on its own until asked for a reason—if you pulled that out in the first sentence, you might come off like you're being condescending, but this way it's just self defence and a valid, mature reason.

Remember: don't be rude! They're within their rights (perhaps not legal rights, but rights nonetheless) to do whatever it is they're doing, and you are well within your rights to say no. You just have to be clear and calm about why not, and keep a smile on your face to prevent misinterpretation.

Try not to get too defensive or upset. If you react too strongly, your friend will most likely realise they've pushed you too far, but back off with a line like 'Jeez, nothing to cry about, I was only asking'—and then you look like an idiot. Deep breaths!

End the Temptation

At some points it might feel easier just to say yes and live with it, but you'll not only feel better for sticking to your beliefs, your friends will respect you too.

If a friend is pushing you too much and not accepting your reasons why you're not interested, come back at him or her—laugh, and say 'Why do you care so much?', or 'What, can't you smoke on your own?' Embarrass them a little and they'll back off.

If that doesn't work, just walk away. Say 'Sorry, it's still a no!' and just turn around. You might be able to use an excuse; say 'I love this song, I'm going to go dance' or something else appropriate. Just remove yourself from the situation. It's important to be clear, and walking away sends a powerful message.

Make it Cool

Don't be embarrassed about your choice. Make it part of who you are. If people are curious about why you say no to a particular thing, be open and honest with them, and don't be too serious about it. You never know which boy might find your choices really attractive. Don't worry if people disagree with you; we're all different, and that's a good thing!

Saying No To ...

AN INVITATION

If you don't want to go to a party or out with someone, that's your right. Saying so can be harder, though! It sounds difficult, but being brutally honest can often be your best bet. Say simply, 'I'm really sorry, I'm just way too tired to come out tonight. Have a great time though!' They might argue a little, which you'll have to live with, but the benefit of being honest is that you don't have to keep up the lie. If you said 'I'm going out with my parents' and then they saw you online all night, you'll have to explain yourself. There's nothing wrong with being too tired, or too sick, or working the next day—you don't have to come to everything!

TELEMARKETERS

Be polite, but firm. No harm saying 'No thanks, I already have that service and it's great' and if they push it, just say 'Sorry, that's the doorbell' and hang up. Sometimes they'll get rude—if they're being smart with you, you could reply 'I was considering it, but your attitude leaves a little to be desired so I've changed my mind'—but say it in a nice tone, otherwise you're just being rude too! If you really can't get them to leave you alone, hang up and block the number.

SEX

Be clear—don't just laugh and say 'stop', they might think you're flirting. Clearly say 'I don't want to do this right now, sorry' and say why. There's no shame in not being ready. If they push you too far, they don't really care about you. If you need to, get up and walk away. Just make sure you can't be misunderstood!

How to Host
A GREAT SLEEPOVER

One of the best bits about having close friends in high school is the sleepover! You can get your closest (or not so close) friends together and bond. The secret to having a great sleepover is being prepared, but not being a control freak. Have lots of options ready, but don't stress if the night doesn't go exactly how you planned!

Get thinking

First you need a purpose for your sleepover. Not necessarily a reason, but a theme. Is it a movie night? A beauty evening of makeup and manicures? A dinner party, gossip evening, or even a night to help somebody get over a break-up? You are more likely to hold a good sleepover if your guests know what to expect.

When inviting people, pick them carefully. Choose friends that get along—it can be good also to have people who don't know each other too well; you'll be surprised how much you all bond. Sleepovers will always work best with all girls, or mostly girls with one or two boys who are sensitive to their feminine sides! It's usually better to hold a party if you want to invite boys. Sleepovers, sadly, are and always will be a girly thing.

Check with your parents. Make sure they understand you'll probably be awake and talking half the night, because it can be really embarrassing if they appear unexpectedly and tell you all to shut up! Explain politely that you'd appreciate if they stayed hidden for the night.

Get ready

You may need to start preparing for your sleepover a few days beforehand to make sure you have everything you need. Depending on your friends, different things can be fun, but there are a few classics that will always be needed at a sleepover!

You'll need:

- space! A big, parent-free room is ideal, or clean up your bedroom with lots of places to sit.
- things to do. Stack up magazines, have makeup and clothes within reach, turn on your computer, charge your camera, put music on and give a choice of movies.
- beds in the same room. Nothing kills the night faster than when you all go off to separate rooms—the best sleepover allows you to be in bed, and still chatting.
- good food! If you're supplying dinner, make it group-friendly like pizza. Have lots of dessert and movie foods handy. Don't forget juice and fizzy drinks, or get creative and make mocktails.

Get started

Try these ideas to make your sleepover unforgettably awesome.

Have a friend (or two) help you plan the night. They'll have ideas you might not have considered, and they can help you shop and set up.

As a change from fizzy drinks and juice, you can try Maison or other non-alcoholic labels that look and taste like wine. Use wine glasses for added class. Better yet, get some recipes off the internet and have fun making mocktails (non-alcoholic cocktails)!

Have an older sibling or parent drive you all to the shops to pick movies together.

Keep a camera handy, in plain view and fully charged. Before long you'll have a zillion awesome photos on it—and what girl doesn't love to model?

Invite your guests over for dinner and stock up on small size pizza bases and ingredients—each of your guests can make their own mini pizza with their favourite toppings to eat while you watch movies. It solves the problem of what to serve for dinner, and they're a lot of fun to make!

Play Truth or Dare. It sounds typical, but it can be so much fun. A twist on the game is playing a Truth or Dare/Spin the Bottle combination, where you spin the bottle to work out who's creating the Dare, and who's doing it!

Short on cash? Have all your friends over and hold a mass makeup and clothes swap. This doesn't even have to be done at night—you won't spend a cent and you'll feel like you went shopping.

If you're stuck for game ideas, hit the internet. Even a poker night can be fun—play with Monopoly money so you can have fun without feeling broke the next day.

Have a horror movie night. Get some popcorn, dim the lights, and try not to be the first one to scream! These nights are perfect for Halloween, or in the winter when it's cold enough for blankets, and pitch black outside.

Try a beauty night—buy some products, and have your friends bring their favourites. Give each other facials, manicures and makeovers and finish the night with the best chick flicks you can find.

Make sure you have loads of food, and give your guests a quick tour so they don't get lost looking for the bathroom!

If you're still awake at 5am, do yoga while the sun rises.

Clean up afterwards. If your parents held a party and expected you to clean for them, you wouldn't be happy about it, so do the right thing! It won't take you long, especially if your friends lend a hand before going home!

62

If in doubt ... get more pillows!

Why Is My Friend ... ?

shutting me down all the time?

She makes me feel stupid for anything I say.

Believe it or not: she's insecure.

The reason she's picking on you in small ways is because she's jealous. You say something, your other friends laugh, she wonders why she didn't think of the joke first. She might pull the 'that's really inappropriate' card: if she says that, first consider if your joke or comment *was* inappropriate—if

you can't work out why, ask! Say 'How is that inappropriate?'. Chances are her answer will be really weak.

Don't play her game. It's tempting to snap back at her, but nothing will annoy her more than realising you really don't care what she thinks. Display your security proudly: let her know you like who you are. It'll teach her a lesson quickly.

sucking up to someone ?

Kim never liked That Band, until the ultra-cool Andrea decided she did. Suddenly, Kim's favourite band is ... ? You guessed it—That Band! Annoying, right?

Funny how just a few weeks ago when you said you loved That Band's new album, Kim said 'As if, they suck!' Feel free to gently remind Kim about this, but don't make too much of a big deal about it. Kim clearly worships Andrea, which is why she's

agreeing with her—to get her approval. Naturally, that's annoying, but it won't be long before Andrea gets annoyed by it too, and if Andrea's as secure as she seems, she'll soon get so annoyed by Kim copying her every choice that she'll tell her to go find some opinions of her own.

In the meantime, be quietly confident in your own security, and sit back, watch and enjoy the 'Kim and Andrea' show! Popcorn, anyone?

mad at me ?

This always sucks, especially when you don't know what it is you did!

If you're not sure what you did, you could ask around. See if any of your friends know why she's mad at you. It could be something small which grew.

If someone told her that you'd been bitching about her, and it's true, the best thing you can do is damage control. Approach her, be honest, bite the bullet and apologise. She can't be mad at you if you're standing there saying 'I know what I did and I was wrong'.

If you still can't work out what's wrong, you could ask her—gently!—or just let it go. Sometimes we all get a little bit sick of each other; she could be PMSing, or if it's a guy, maybe he has a secret crush on you and he's acting mad to hide it! Just leave it for a few days and it might go away.

In the meantime, give your friend space, and be nice but not needy. Eventually they'll give you a sign that they're not mad anymore, like a hug or a compliment—thank them casually so they know it's all okay.

THE
Best Friends
QUIZ

How close are you, really? Photocopy this page, take the quiz, mark each other's answers and find out ...

My best friend's ...	*Is ...*
Hair colour:	
Birthday:	
Middle name:	
Favourite colour:	
Favourite band:	
Favourite school subject:	
Favourite activity:	
Celebrity crush:	
Real-life crush:	
Dream job:	
Final Mark:	

Buying perfect presents

It's next to impossible to get a good present, especially when you're buying for a guy. Here are some ideas for the perfect gift for that annoying friend who always says 'I don't want anything!'

'She's in my grade but I don't know her very well'

Try beauty products such as bath bombs, body lotion and makeup. If you've got some money to spare, buy a clutch purse and fill it with small items or cosmetics such as nail polish, and little chocolates. You could also try CD or clothing vouchers, trinket boxes, jewellery, photo frames, chocolate or wind chimes.

'She's my best friend—but she said "no presents"'

If you want to buy her a gift, do it! Bake her a cake if she'll get mad at you for spending money. Otherwise, try a nice necklace, charm bracelet or clothes. If you're not sure of her style, buy her pyjamas! If you're creative, gather photos of the two of you and make a collage, scrapbook or photo album. Make her a box filled with things you love about her: glue a photo of her onto the lid and fill the box with symbols of her personality. Get creative! All you need is paper and glue. And just remember: failing those ideas, chocolate always works.

'He's a good friend, but guys are so hard to buy for!'

Vouchers are nearly always the best way to go with a guy. If you know a little more about him you could try a CD, nice wallet, watch or belt, or a book or movie. Otherwise, try something silly that references a running joke, bake him a cake, or just drown him in chocolate.

Ben's dream birthday gift is 'to have the best night ever, with everybody I invited to turn up'.

If you can't throw a party, what about a barbeque at the local lake, a shopping trip or a day at the movies? You could even throw him or her a surprise dinner—if everyone pays for themselves and then chips in for your friend's dinner, it needn't cost anyone too much and you'll all have a great night out.

Gift Hampers

Buy a nice basket or box and throw together little things for a thoughtful gift that they'll love.

Summer survival box: beach towel, fake tan, bright nail polish, sunglasses, dress.

City style box: heels (or voucher!), sunglasses, hair accessories, jewellery, clutch purse, eyeliner.

Relaxation box: bath gel, chill-out CD, body lotion, scented candles, eye mask, incense.

Winter warmer box: marshmallows, hot chocolate, slippers, a good DVD and a cute pair of earmuffs!

EMBRACING
your differences

How to make being the 'odd one out' one of the best things that ever happened to you.

You're clumsy, or you hate your freckles, you're the only blonde in your group ... it's weird how the little things can make the biggest differences between you and your friends. You might feel like it's not okay to be the only one in your group who doesn't like a particular band, but guess what? It's one of the coolest things about you.

Why it pays to be different

Think of your coolest friend. She's not perfect—nobody is. But in your eyes, it might not seem like she has ANY flaws, right? Wrong. If you ask her, she'll immediately say she hates her nose, or she feels like her laugh is weird. No doubt you've never noticed any of those things, and you know why? Because she's learnt how to work with them.

If you take what's different about you and make it your signature trait, it stops being awkward or embarrassing. It becomes cool. You might know a girl with a hilarious habit for knocking things over— she laughs, you laugh, nobody judges her. She

might have considered herself clumsy and it could have led to really low self-esteem, but feeling down on yourself isn't worth it for something like that! Make it your 'thing'. Make it the thing that everyone describes you by: 'You know, Madison, the one who laughs like a hyena!' Nobody minds that you laugh like a hyena—it doesn't offend anybody—so why be upset about it? Laugh as much as you can and let everybody know that you're the girl with the totally unique honking noise.

Change your approach

Next time you see red roots coming through your carefully dyed hair, don't run for the hairdresser's. Let them grow out. You'll be amazed how many people say 'Wow! You should dye your hair red all the time'—you'll also be surprised when you realise nobody even knew your hair was red because you've been hiding the differences all along.

You don't know what people will say until you show off your 'flaw'— what do you have to lose?

when *friends* become enemies

You were friends for life. You knew each other inside and out, you made jokes, you stuck up for one another in arguments. All of a sudden, she's turned on you, and you don't know why. So what happens when friends become enemies?

There are a million and one reasons for why. It could be that you've done something to offend her. She might just be having a bad day. Or she's completely insane and she's decided you've been trying to steal her boyfriend. Ultimately, when it comes to these situations, the reason doesn't even matter. If she wants to be mad at you, she will be.

Talk About It

Not easy, but absolutely necessary—talk about it. If you know why she's mad and you owe her an apology—give it to her. Have the courage to approach her at lunch and take her aside, say 'I'm really sorry,' and don't make excuses. Nine times out of ten, you'll be friends again within a week.

If you don't know what you've done, or if you've just drifted apart, there are a few things you can do. You can try to make contact casually—such as a comment on Facebook about something else—and see how she responds, or you can give it some time and leave her to make up her own mind about whether or not she wants to be your friend.

When You're the Enemy

If you're just thoroughly sick of your friend, or you don't think you can forgive her for what she did, you might choose to take some time. You're allowed to do this—it can be difficult, but you're within your rights to decide who you want as a friend. However, as someone you used to trust, she deserves an explanation as to why. Be clear about why you feel hurt, and give her the chance to apologise. Try not to be too nasty—when you want to be friends again, she might not feel the same way if you've been cruel! Just clearly state that she's hurt your feelings and you need some time and space.

When You're in the Same Group

It might make being in the same group awkward if you're giving each other the silent treatment. Try not to drag your friends into it: no nasty gossip, and no ultimatums like 'If she's coming to your party, I'm not'! Respect that they have nothing to do with the argument, and keep them out of it.

EDIT YOUR IMAGE

It's important to know who you are, and to like yourself. The cool thing about being comfortable in your own skin, is that once you know who you are, you can work on improving yourself. Here are some quick and easy ways to be the girl who ...

... tells great stories

Being entertaining can be a really useful skill.

- Stories that offend or embarrass others, or racist, homophobic and sexist stories, are a definite no. Unless it's about how a racist got shut down, or something similar, it's thin ice.
- Don't plan the moment. Stories are best when they're within the conversation's topic. Otherwise you'll look like you scripted it.
- Self-deprecating, confession style stories are often the funniest. Pick your audience, though—girls may laugh at how you caught the cat playing with a tampon but the guys might just feel uncomfortable!
- Everybody strays from truth a little, but people can pick all-out lies and nobody likes a liar. If you do take it away from the strict truth, don't take it too far!
- Don't become a laughter addict. When the story's over, it's over. If you keep trying to expand it, it will die. Enjoy the laughter while you have it! Don't hog the conversation with your stories. Share the limelight.
- Laugh with everyone. Be animated. Enjoy it!

... leads the grade

Confidence and accessibility are all you need.

- Take any opportunity to make a speech or organise an event. However, don't fight too hard for that chance—give other people a go!
- Join the Student Representative Council and ask a wide cross-section of your grade what they think about certain issues. Hear and act on their opinions. Help them be heard.
- Wear the school uniform with pride, but add quirky touches (such as a cool bag or interesting hairstyles) to express yourself.
- If you're representing the SRC, in speeches tell your grade that they can come to you with any questions. Make it about them, not you.
- Attend lots of grade social outings so that people know you're not obsessed with school and that you enjoy your social life too.

... everybody loves

The trick to this is that it's not actually about getting people to like you. It's about showing them your awesome side.

This takes energy because you need loads of patience and positivity. Try the following tips and see how quickly you'll develop a following:

- Laugh. Lots! Laugh at the worst jokes and the best ones. More importantly, learn to laugh at yourself. If you're the butt of a joke and you get mad, you're just going to make it funnier—or awkward—for everybody else. Learn to see the funny side in your mistakes.
- Have your own opinions. Don't force them on people, but don't be afraid to disagree—in a friendly way. If they're all chatting about how awesome a movie was and you disagree, say 'That's so weird, because I hated it! Am I missing something?' It'll draw you into the conversation while still allowing you your own opinion.
- Don't be exclusive. Get to know the 'nerds' just as well as the 'popular' group. Smile and say hi to everyone from new students to teachers and even the principal. Friendly is way more interesting and attractive than exclusive.
- Leave some mystery. Talk about yourself a little, but bounce the conversation back to the other person as much as possible. Relate to them, actually listen, and follow up the story later. Wouldn't you come to love the girl who remembered your piano recital was on Saturday and wished you luck, even though you only mentioned it in passing?

... shines with beauty

Everybody's gorgeous in their own right. Any professional photographer will tell you that. The trick is how to get that out of yourself on a day-to-day basis.

- The important thing is to avoid narcissism. Your personality is more important—and should be as attractive—as your looks.
- Learn to dress for your figure. Hippie is a better look for curvy girls than tight-fitting clothes. The city look works for a lot of girls. Buy clothes and accessories that work for you. Size is irrelevant—if you look hotter in 12 than 10, wear 12!
- Don't cake on the makeup! Fake eyebrows and two inches of foundation will only freak people out. Light or no foundation and natural, minimal makeup looks best for school.
- Hairstyles say a lot: a tightly gathered bun sends a completely different message to a sporty ponytail, which in turn gives a different idea to long, thick, curly hair, worn out and free. Find four hairstyles that work with your hair, experiment, and don't be afraid to do nothing at all with it.
- Carefree beauty is so attractive. A girl who freely gets involved in a water fight is much prettier than the one who shrieks and yells 'Don't! You'll ruin my fake tan!'. Guys don't really care if you're pale. But they'll definitely notice if you're high-maintenance!
- Get lots of sleep. Eight hours of sleep and no makeup trumps six hours sleep and perfect makeup. Energetic personalities are enchanting. Let your natural beauty shine.
- Stop caring what people think. Easier said than done, yes, but wear that skirt you think you're 'too fat' for and wear it with confidence. You'll be surprised at the amount of compliments you'll get!

10 Things ...
TO DO BEFORE YOU DIE
Taken from a blog post from January 2009

1. Go overseas
Top of the list, this one! Doesn't matter where you go or what you do there, just go overseas. Do some day tours and party at night. Take a group tour and meet people. It doesn't matter—just being overseas is the most incredible experience, you learn so much about life and culture—and you learn a lot about your own culture, comparing it to someone else's. Actually, while we're on this, I should add:

2. Be an exchange student
Now, I know this one's a bit harder but it's a great, cheap way to see another country, and it's amazing for confidence! I truly believe that the best way to find out who you are is to leave everything else behind, and being an exchange student is such a great way to do that. The experiences I gained have changed my life. And, you can kill points 1 and 2 just by doing this!

3. Speak in front of an audience
Did you know that more people fear public speaking than death? I still get nervous talking, even when it's just on assembly when nobody's actually listening! But it's a really good skill to have, public speaking/microphone work—it'll help heaps if you ever get a job where you have to make presentations, and learning

how to fake confidence has really helped me in some tricky situations! Plus, and this is going to sound SO nerdy—the adrenaline is great. It's a performance, and the thrill of performance is totally underrated.

4. Ride a rollercoaster

Three years ago, I'd never have said this one. And it's one of those things that too many people get scared of too easily. Again, the thrill is excellent. And if you only do it once and decide you hate it, at least it's one more experience for the list!

5. Do some volunteer or charity work

Yeah, I know, that sounds both weird and unappealing, but the karma's all there. And I know that's not helping the cause here, but the thing is, doing charity work helped me realise how many uncharitable people there are in the world. And when you find a charitable person, the feeling is great.

6. Do something unbelievably stupid

Doesn't matter what it is, as long as it embarrasses the hell out of you! Why? Because it's okay to look like an idiot and once you embrace that, life's so much more fun. Dye your hair! Sing in the street, dance in the shops, run around in the park! Especially for people of my nerd calibre, being an idiot sometimes is a great release.

7. Witness a breathtaking sight

The Grand Canyon, the pyramids, the view from the London Eye, a celebrity in Hollywood, the Cerne Abbas man, those giant chalk drawing things near Peru, the Mona Lisa, Niagara Falls, Uluru, Petra, Vatican City's amazing architecture, sunsets and sunrises, a completely undisturbed lagoon in Fiji ... or simply a bird preening its feathers in your own backyard.

8. See a musical or some other kind of really big show

Get on a theatre website and book for anything that catches your eye. The costumes, sets, music (of course) and acting in a professional musical/'really big show' is breathtaking! And you always leave the theatre feeling so great. Trust me. Money well spent.

9. Be a tourist in your own town

The thing is, locals are almost at a disadvantage—living in the area, we're used to it and so we don't tend to do all the 'tourist' things! So if you go into your nearest city with the eyes of a newcomer, some of the things you'll get to see and do are truly awesome. I wonder how many Londoners have bothered with a Thames river cruise? See what I mean? You don't tend to look at your home city with those eyes, but you find out so much more if you play traveller for the day.

10. Pick up a new skill

So often we say 'I'd love to know how to ...', or 'I want to be able to ...' and yet we never take the steps to actually do it. Just learning to drive is damn near impossible, who has the time to take a class? But if you do decide to find the time and take the class, who knows where that skill might take you, the fun you'll have, and the people you'll meet along the way? Take a weekend workshop—go with a friend, parent or sibling for the added bonus of a little bonding.

getting the party started

Yay! It's your birthday. Or Christmas. Or Halloween. Or Friday night. You don't really need an excuse to throw a party: they're great no matter what they're for! But it's hard to decide what kind of party to throw. Check out the options below and see what suits you, or take bits of each and go totally unique. Have fun!

classic and crowded

Suitable for: if you have parents who don't mind how many people you have over.

The gist: make some punch, get a loud stereo, and set up your back deck with lights. Invite practically everyone in your grade and have a very rowdy, loud, social night.

How to pull it off: the basis of this party is good music, and lots of different food and drink will help your guests have a great night! Get some friends to help out with your playlist, clear some areas away for dancing, and make sure there are lots of cushions, chairs and couches for people to chill out. Make sure you invite lots of people, too—these nights don't work with small groups.

What to expect: they'll explore your whole house and you'll be cleaning for years, but it'll be fun!

girls' night in

Suitable for: if you only want a small group or you aren't allowed boys over or a big party.

The gist: buy makeup, ice cream, girly movies. Set your lounge room up with mattresses and cushions and spend the night in your pyjamas, painting each others' toenails and watching movies.

How to pull it off: you need good movies, good food, and plenty of space. If your lounge room is small, only invite two or three friends. Make sure the girls you invite all like each other, and keep it quiet so nobody gets upset that they weren't invited. Have pizza for dinner and get lots of dessert. You could even play a game like Twister or Truth or Dare.

What to expect: you'll talk all night and share plenty of secrets. It's a great way to bond.

costume party

Suitable for: outgoing friends and parents who don't mind how much money you spend.

The gist: set a theme, decorate as such, and tell everyone to come in costume of that theme.

How to pull it off: firstly, pick a cool theme that people can get costumes for, cheaply! Try 1920s, or cartoon characters, or accept any kind of costume, so long as they dress up. Then, decorate with the theme. If it's a Halloween party, hang little skeletons from the doorframes and make 'creepy' food. If it's a celebrities party, put stars on the doors like change rooms, lay down a red carpet and get the cameras going like paparazzi!

What to expect: the photos will be absolutely hilarious, but a few friends might wimp out.

Whatever you do, do NOT put the party details online! Private messages only. Play it safe.

ten toptips about socialising

BE YOURSELF! It's easy. People can tell when you're pretending to be something you're not, and it's not going to win you any friends because in the end it's just annoying. Be proud of who you are!

It's easy to be a bitch on the internet—we all feel braver behind the keyboard. However, before you type that nasty comment, think how you'd feel if someone said it to you. Just keep it positive.

Get your friends to help out with your next party—having them help with decorations, music, food and drinks will make the whole night better for everyone. Get some fresh eyes on your ideas!

You don't need to invite 100 people to have a great night. Try a girls' night in: make dinner, watch a movie, gossip till the sun rises. Have a beauty night or a scrapbooking party—try something new.

If you suspect your friend has taken too much of something, call an ambulance! You're not a paramedic, so don't trust your own diagnosis. Just do something about it. Don't risk the alternative.

Set reminders on your phone a few days before friends' birthdays. That way you'll never have to suffer the guilt of forgetting, and you'll be the awesome friend who even had time to write a card!

If your friend is stressing WAY too much about school, casually mention another friend and say how cool it is that she doesn't stress. Your freak-out friend will soon realise she's being too much.

When a friend's going through a breakup, whether the relationship lasted for 3 years or 3 days, be there for her, unconditionally. Even if you hated the guy—wouldn't she support you if you were upset?

On your own at a party? Go up to a group of people and say so. Just be honest and friendly and they'll be happy to include you in their conversation. Much better than standing awkwardly by the food all night, right?

It's very easy to be offended by something someone says—but it's a much better revenge not to let it get to you. If they're trying to upset you and you just accept it—or better yet, laugh and agree with their insult—they'll lose all their power. Refuse to be a victim!

love
life

These years are home to a lot of firsts. You'll probably have your first kiss. You might have sex for the first time. One relationship doesn't mean you're an expert at them all; the tips inside this chapter will help you avoid common pitfalls of teenage relationships.

LOVE YOURSELF:
Love Someone Else

ben says

" I love a girl with confidence but no cockiness, and I love intelligence but I prefer sense of humour the most because I'm the kind of person who is always in a good mood, and love people who can take a joke.

Confidence is attractive; girls should like who they are. If she's pretending, then she's basically a drama student and she's acting all the time; I don't like the actress type. Secondly, if she's acting how she thinks I want her to be, then she could be thinking wrongly and have different expectations, so I would never get to see what she's actually like! "

Every school has a girl like this. The one where she used to be your best friend. She was funny, spontaneous, secure in herself, and liked going out. And now she's with a boyfriend and she's a completely different person. She doesn't even claim to like the same music. Even her dream job has changed. Suddenly she's a clone of him. It's sickening to watch, and it's really unhealthy.

Girls like this can be really frustrating because often they're so much fun when they're single, but now you feel like you just don't know them anymore. You want to grab them and yell 'You were great how you were! Why change?!'.

Why change, indeed? The reason these girls mould to their boyfriends is because they're insecure. They don't believe they have anything to offer, and they're obsessed with the idea that once their boyfriends discover who they really are, they'll be bored and leave. So they change everything about themselves.

There's not much you can do in a situation like this without putting your friendship at risk. You can gently remind your friend that she had plenty of friends while she was single, but go too straightforward and she'll be really offended. What you can do, however, is learn a lesson.

If you don't love yourself, nobody else can love you. These girls, 9 times out of 10, end up getting ditched by their boyfriends because the boy feels like it's not a challenge, or that she's not the girl he used to like. That's the whole point: if they start dating you in the first place, they must like you as you are, so why change?

Hopefully she'll realise she's lost too many friends, and she'll learn her own lesson. Meanwhile, you have to practise loving yourself and when you pick up an awesome guy that you can be yourself around, she'll realise what she's missing. And you'll be really, truly happy. Does sacrificing everything you are sound like happiness? Hell no. Be yourself. The rest is easy.

Being yourself is easier said than done, but when you find a partner who sees the real you and likes it—you'll know it was worth the effort.

77

the Crush Guide

There's nothing like the feeling of a crush. That guy you didn't really care about three days ago is suddenly catching your eye, and class is useless because you're too busy writing his name in hearts in your notebook … what you need right now is the guide to getting the guy!

WHEN HE'S GOT A GIRLFRIEND ...

You might hate to hear this, but there's nothing you can do. If he's got a girlfriend, he's completely off-limits. You can still dream! By all means, enjoy what's in your head, but don't act on it. No flirting. No being mean to his girlfriend. And NO trying to break them up! Think how you'd feel if someone was trying to steal away your boyfriend—it's totally undignified and definitely not worth the drama!

WHEN HE'S FREE AND SINGLE

You might be scared, but it's worth a try if you really like this guy. Take a deep breath, put on your best 'I'm confident' face, and look to the right for some genius ideas on getting the guy!

STEP ONE: STOP FAKING IT!

Guess what? Boys don't really stop and stare when you strut past them in heels and flick your hair. That sort of drama is reserved for the movies. Any guy will tell you they prefer someone who'll be able to hold a conversation, even if it's you listening while they talk about video games. So just be yourself! If they don't like you for who you are, they're idiots anyway and aren't worth your time. You want someone who likes you for you, otherwise what's the point?

STEP TWO: GET FABULOUS

That being said, as long as you're being yourself, there's no harm in feeling great about how you look and who you are. Paint your nails or try a different hairstyle for a confidence boost. You're already gorgeous, you just need to know you are! But don't change your entire look to what you *think* he'll like; chances are he thought you were pretty anyway, and guys don't like high-maintenance girls. If he compliments you on looking nice, don't say 'No, I look terrible!' because guys don't respond well to that. Just thank him graciously and change the subject. Or, look a little surprised, say 'Really?' and when he says yes, say 'Thank you, that's really nice!' He'll feel good for flattering you and he'll know you can take a compliment.

STEP THREE: TEST THE WATERS

Does your friend know him? Ask her what he's like, what he's into, and things he likes to do. If you have a regular excuse to talk to him (say, you share a lab bench in Science), then take it. Be friendly and open, but don't be clingy. If you're approaching him every lunch time and not giving him any time with his friends, he'll soon get a bit weirded out. Stay a little mysterious. You want him curious.

STEP FOUR: TAKE IT OUTSIDE

Just like in all the movies, crushes blossom most wonderfully outside of school. There's nothing romantic about Maths. See if you can end up at the same party as him, and be friendly and confident but not too pushy. Resist the urge to draw him in by complaining—he might comfort you about your dog running away for half an hour, but if you're doing it every day he's just going to think you're hating life. Not sexy.

If he's not showing any interest in you by this point, it might be time to step back from the situation. But if he's making the effort to talk to you (see the next page for details!) then it's definitely worth a shot. Let things progress naturally by flirting, or be bold and tell him you like him. Be prepared for a rejection, no matter how you approach it! A good rule of thumb is that if you're not sure he's interested, wait longer, and give him some space. Have faith in yourself—you deserve a good guy!

DOES HE LIKE YOU?

So, you talk to each other, you laugh ... and you like him so much it makes you want to cry. Sound familiar? Want to know if he feels the same way? Read on!

Read the Clues

Firstly, you need to look and listen. You might find yourself talking to him regularly, but how does that happen?

What you're really looking for is effort on his part. For example, you text and talk, but what you're looking for is if he texts you first, or if he approaches you at school. Does he make the effort to begin a conversation with you?

When you're actually in conversation with him, look for clues that he wants to continue talking. Does he ask questions he's already asked, invite you places, and laugh even when your jokes aren't funny?

Experiment: If you always text him at 7pm, stop. Wait and see if he texts you once he realises the text he's come to expect isn't happening tonight. If he texts you, it's a good sign he enjoys your conversation!

Body Language

Boys say more through what they do, than what they say—we all know women can talk until the sun goes down, but men speak loudest through actions.

In conversation, does he really pay attention to

'Women can talk until the sun goes down, but men speak loudest through actions.'

every word you're saying? Is he making constant eye contact, laughing a lot, and standing close?

Look for stance signals such as his arms—if they're folded, he's protecting himself. If they're relaxed and open, he trusts you.

Does he tickle you, pretend to punch you or make excuses to touch you ('er, I'm just fixing your collar there'—sure, sure!) in conversation? These are all surefire signs that at the very least, you've made yourself a good friend, or he's totally into you.

Experiment: When he makes a joke, laugh and gently touch him on the arm while laughing or telling him how funny he is. Watch for his reaction. Is he pleased you touched and complimented him? Does he then make an excuse to touch or compliment you in return?

Every Guy is Different

You might feel he's giving you all the signals, and he'll surprise you by telling you he has a girlfriend. Or, you'll give up hope, thinking his body language is so closed off, and the next day he'll ask you out! It's far from an exact art and you have to be brave. *The best way to find out will always be to ask!*

I know you wanted answers, so I asked Ben for the guy's view. Read on for some surprising guy secrets ...

What do guys do to show a girl they like them?

ben says

"Well there's a lot of answers for this! I'll tell you what I do and what people I know do.

To show a girl I like her, first of all I give her attention. Probably take a different approach to talk to her—compliment her smile, or maybe her hair or perfume. Spend time with her and maybe buy her a gift every now and then, and make her feel at home when she's at mine.
There's a lot I do to show a girl I like her but it depends who it is because different things impress different people, but I mainly try to make them laugh or smile.
And the main thing: when they're talking, I look at them or into their eyes to show I'm interested in what they have to say.

Some people I know try to buy love—they'll spend a lot of money but that's silly, because those guys always get used.

Some guys are horrible to girls they like. This is the stupidest thing that I usually witness! I can't see how being horrible shows you like a person, it's dumb."

Asking HIM OUT

So you've completed the crush guide, you're confident he likes you, and you can talk to him freely. If you're feeling confident that you're on the edge of a relationship, but he just doesn't seem to be keen on making that first move ... why don't you do it? Break the gender stereotype and ask him out first.

Ben has never, not once in his life, asked out a girl. And yet he's been in plenty of relationships. He thinks that 'all that nonsense about guys having to be the ones who ask girls out, makes me laugh. How I see it, is if you like someone, then ask them out.' Simple as that.

Simple, but scary, right? He doesn't disagree. Ben's main reason for not asking girls out is 'you never know if they only say yes to make you feel better'—that's just how sweet girls are, apparently! So, there you have it. Guys are scared too. They have the exact same doubts and fears that girls have when it comes to making a connection official, and why not? It's a scary thing to do. And no matter how prepared

you feel, it'll probably still be scary. But it's like ripping off a Band-Aid. You just have to go for it.

Opportunity

Don't put yourself through the extra stress of asking out a guy in front of all his mates, or a classroom full of people. It's definitely not worth the panic!

Wait for a time when you're alone together (even if it means saying 'Can I talk to you for a second?' and pulling him aside) so you can speak freely.

If you're the nervous type, there's nothing wrong with asking him online. If you usually chat online then it doesn't have to be awkward. Even by text is fine; again, if you talk like that normally. If you never text and then his first text from you is asking him out, he might be really surprised. It's much less nerve-racking if he's expecting it!

Conversation

You can walk straight up to him and ask him out if you want—it shows that you're confident and not afraid to speak your mind. But if the thought of starting a conversation with that question makes your knees turn to jelly, you could always just gear the chat towards the idea.

For example, ask him if he's into anyone lately, or tell him you have a party coming up and everyone's bringing boyfriends. Get the conversation to a point where it's the next logical step to ask. This is a lot easier online because you have a chance to think about what you'll say, and phrase it well, but it can work face-to-face too.

Sometimes, if he likes you and he's confident, your gearing the conversation towards the question can lead to him asking you! Consider yourself lucky if that happens, and say yes with a smile.

Preparation

Have the sentence ready ('Will you go out with me?' 'So, how would you feel about being my boyfriend?') so you don't stumble over your words. Make sure you smile, or ask it in a friendly tone—sometimes girls come off as really blunt when they're nervous!

Most importantly, be prepared for the chance that he might say no. Try to take it gracefully if he does—if he says no and you go psycho, it's 99% certain that the next big story around the school is how crazy you are when you're turned down! Just take a deep breath, smile, and say 'Well, worth a shot' or 'That's a shame', and walk away. If he's really rude with his rejection then he's not worth your time anyway. Make sure you have a friend ready in case things go wrong, or to celebrate with if it goes well!

Saying NO

So, he's asked you, and he's last on your list of dateable guys? Definitely awkward. Here's how to defuse the situation and leave him feeling as good as possible.

Firstly, smile. It's a compliment that he likes you—if you're creeped out, hide it! Say something like, 'wow, it's really nice that you think of me like that, and thank you so much ...' and then follow it with the truth: diplomat style. Tell him what you really think but say it in nice words!

'... but I'm really not looking for a boyfriend right now. I just want to have fun with my friends and be single.'

'... but I really think of you as a good friend and I don't want to ruin that. Relationships threaten friendships.'

'... but I'm actually sort of with someone right now. Just bad timing, I guess.'

Finish with 'I'm sorry, I hope we're all good' but don't beg if he gets mad. You're within your rights to say no, and he has to handle that! Just try to phrase it so he doesn't feel too rejected, and it'll all be fine eventually. If he gets angry, remove yourself from the situation politely—be friendly and casual, but log offline, leave the room or walk away.

The Dating Game

So, you're seeing someone! There's nothing more exciting than a new relationship in high school. But it's easy to slip into a 'see each other at school' routine and never actually be a couple outside of that. Time to play the dating game …

When you're outside of school with a new boyfriend or girlfriend, it's often a bit awkward. You're used to seeing each other at lunchtimes, surrounded by friends, and suddenly it's 'real'! Especially if it's a serious date—just the two of you—it can feel like pretty unfamiliar territory. But there are ways to make it more comfortable and more fun. Just check out the next page for killer date material!

Try some of these ideas:

- Make a conscious effort to be positive. Often when people are nervous they come off as sullen—you don't want him to think you don't like him or you're bored!
- Go somewhere non-threatening, like aqua golf, the movies or bowling. A romantic dinner for two might be a little intimidating, so early on in your relationship!
- Dates where conversation comes easily are the best. In other words, if you have him or her over to your house, make sure you have something to do like watch a movie or play a game. If you're relying on having something to talk about for four hours, it could get awkward.
- Seeing a movie is an awesome date for romance. You can see a horror and cuddle into his chest, or choose a romantic film and you might just find yourselves kissing as the screen couple do. You can talk about the movie on the way home, and avoid all awkward silences.
- Be yourself! You've probably heard it a million times but you need to believe it. If he or she is dating you, then they like you as you are.
- Don't order a salad and then lust after his steak—guys find that really annoying. If you want to eat lots, do it!
- Dress nice, but try not to show off too much skin. A 'hippie' look is often nice; it displays your femininity (which can be very attractive) without being revealing.
- Don't get taken away by the drama. A lot of movies show troubled girls and then display their guys miraculously knowing that something's wrong, actually caring, and working out exactly how to fix it, or just being really supportive. Guess what? Even adult males aren't that intuitive, let alone teenage boys! If you act sulky and try to get him to ask what's wrong, it's almost a guarantee that he'll miss the point altogether and just think you're naturally pretty dull. Don't screw up a good first date just because you're after the 'glamour' of a dramatic relationship. It's honestly not worth it.
- Ask questions! It's the easiest way to make conversation. Whenever there's an awkward silence, ask your date something. It could be simple like 'So, how are you going on that awful Science assignment?' to something crazy like 'So, who would win in a fight, a lion or a crocodile?'

date spots

Where to go and what to do are sometimes impossible decisions for dates. But don't worry—these ideas will have you sorted!

new couples

See a romance or a horror at the cinema—or appeal to his guy side and watch a thriller or action film. Don't forget a big tub of popcorn to share!

Challenge him to aqua golf, putt putt, tennis, or bowling. The element of competition will have you bonding in minutes.

Take him to a barbeque with a few mutual friends. Make sure you both have a wingman in case things get awkward.

strong couples

Pack a nice picnic to share at a quiet lake or cliff. But make sure you tell someone where you're going, especially if it's secluded.

Rent a couple of movies, set the lounge up with lots of pillows and blankets, buy a truckload of food and have a 'winter day in'. If it's summer, put the fan on so you can still snuggle!

Go out to a romantic dinner or lunch—there are plenty of nice places that are cheap enough, and you can play at 'first dates' with a table for two.

Another aspect of the dating game is how much you can learn about a guy within one date. Yep, within just a couple of hours you can find out how compatible you are, where the roadblocks might be and how long you'll last as a couple. All you need is to observe your date closely, and then read on ...

ALWAYS MAKING JOKES

You get home at the end of a date and realise that while you laughed a lot and had a good time ... you didn't exchange a single serious word. Where did all the conversation go?

There are a few reasons why a guy might use too much humour on a date. There's a possibility he's nervous, and his jokes make you laugh which makes him feel more relaxed. He might also be using humour as a way to avoid serious conversation—he might be a bit closed-off. Other than that, he might just be having a really good day where the jokes just keep coming to him!

It's okay to have a date where you don't find out that much about each other. There's time for that. However, on the next date, try asking him a few questions—he might avoid them or combat with humour but be persistent. Even if his answer is in the form of a joke, at least it's an answer! You'll get through to the real him eventually—and maybe the real him is hilarious.

RUDE TO THE WAITRESS

He's polite as anything when he's speaking to you, but he screamed at your waitress for bringing him the wrong soda. Not a good sign!

It's a tried-and-tested trick that if your man's rude to the waitress, he's generally not a good guy. People are people—the woman serving you today

If you can be completely idiotic around each other; you've got something good!

might be waitressing to put herself through university to become a doctor. And even if she's not, even if she's 'just a waitress', she's still a person. Nobody needs to be screamed at over a dirty fork.

If this happens, apologise to the waitress or waiter first. Your boy might be having a bad day and he might immediately feel regretful. But if you ask him about it and he doesn't think he's done anything wrong, or he uses an excuse like 'He's a waiter, what would he know?', run fast. That kind of elitist attitude will be getting him—and consequently, you—into trouble for years. But before you ditch him, tell him why! He needs to know his attitude is a bad one.

STAYS RESPECTFUL

He holds your hand while you're walking, opens doors for you, offers to pay for your ticket or dinner, and kisses you at the end of the date but doesn't try anything else. Translation: he's a keeper!

Boys like this have either been very carefully listening to their big sisters, or they're just naturally smooth. A guy who treats his girl like this on the first date clearly wants a second date, and he's also interested in you—not just getting some action.

Make sure you're appreciative of any guy who acts like this for you. Say 'thank you' lots and make sure you at least pretend to think about declining when he offers to pay for the dinner! If you start to expect these things, you'll stop appearing grateful and he might feel like it's not worth it anymore. Meanwhile, make the most of dating him! Being out with a guy like this can make you feel like a princess. Enjoy it!

VERY COMPETITIVE

If you go to aqua golf and he practically breaks his club in fury when you win, you may need to take a closer look at why.

He might be joking. Competitiveness can be a lot of fun and a good trick for fast bonding. He might be fine, and his anger could be a joke. You can test this by acting like he's kidding when he gets angry—if he gets mad at you for laughing, simply say 'Sorry, I thought you were joking' which will do two things—you'll know for sure that he's a sore loser, and he'll realise his reaction is putting you off.

If he is kidding, you two could have a lot of fun playing games together—challenge him again and see how it goes. But if he isn't joking, consider dates that keep you equal. If you end up in a long-term relationship, his competitiveness is something you can work on together. But for now, while you're just having fun, find ways to have fun that involve either him winning, or no competition at all!

HOW WELL DO YOU KNOW YOUR *boyfriend?*

Do you know your boyfriend as well as you think you do? And how well does he know you?
Photocopy this page, fill in each other's answers and find out!

My partner's ...	Is ...
Birthday:	
Middle name:	
Favourite food:	
Favourite colour:	
Favourite band:	
Favourite school subject:	
Favourite sport:	
Favourite game:	
Favourite date spot:	
Dream job:	
Final Mark:	

Get him thinking: whoever answers the most questions right gets a massage, a free dinner, or a
really good kiss. Work out the prize before you start!

'Well, that's new ...'
WHAT TO DO WHEN
YOUR BODY TRANSFORMS

As you get older, your body will undergo some serious changes to get ready for womanhood and childbearing. These don't need to be scary—think of it as a caterpillar becoming a butterfly, or your superhero self developing. Unfortunately, we can't scientifically call it 'superhero-fying'—it's called puberty, and the stage afterwards is adolescence.

You'll probably know most of this from health classes, adults and friends, so here's a quick guide on what your body's going to be doing over the next few years. No need to freak out—it's all normal, and every stage of puberty happens differently for every person.

'What?!' Moment #1 - you suddenly have breasts.

Breasts, boobs, rack, tits, jugs, whatever you want to call them, there's no denying that they're the all-too-visible mark of a woman! Sadly, we can't choose how big or small they will be or how fast or slow they should grow. We can't tell them when to start growing, or when to stop. What we can do, though, is make sure that they get the right support from the start. Not only does this help stop them becoming saggy and gross as we get older, it also helps with posture and back issues, so as soon as your breasts start to show themselves, get yourself fitted for a bra. And as they grow, make sure you get refitted into bigger bras!

You don't need to be embarrassed of your bras—if none of your friends are wearing them, buy skin-coloured bras so they're less obvious. Or have fun with them—buy nice colours and different styles.

What's normal? Well, almost anything! Your breasts might start growing as early as 8 years of age, or not start until you're 14. And when they do start, they don't normally start together, so don't worry if you wake up one day and notice that one nipple is suddenly bumpy, and sometimes even a bit itchy. It could be that way for a few weeks or more until the other one decides to join in. And even when they do start growing, it's totally normal for one breast to be bigger than the other.

If one breast starts and a year later the other one is still hiding, then it's probably worth checking with the GP just to make sure everything's okay.

'What?!' Moment #2 - you're feeling ape-like ...

Feeling hairy? No, not the hair on your head. The hair under your arms, and ... yep ... between your legs. Pubic hair is a slightly less visible mark of impending womanhood. You will probably find that as your pubic hair starts to grow, the sweat glands under your arms will also suddenly spring to life. If you realise one day that you're not smelling quite as fresh as you used to, then it's probably time to start using underarm deodorant—before you start losing your friends! Many deodorants have chemicals and perfumes in them that might react with your skin, so it's best to start with a gentle, hypo-allergenic one until you know what your skin can take.

You can remove your leg and underarm hair with a razor, by waxing (best to get this done by a professional first—it's hard to pull that first wax strip off yourself!), or using an epilator or hair removal cream. As pubic hair sits on sensitive skin, don't ever use a hair removal cream that isn't strictly designed for that area, and don't epilate! Some girls shave, and others wax—others leave it all natural!

'What?!' Moment #3 - yep, that's your period.

Getting your first period is a 'yes, I'm a woman!' moment, but it also sucks—and a lot of that will depend on your age. Most girls get their first period around the age of 12, but anything between 9 and 14 is quite normal.

A period marks the approach to being able to reproduce—to have babies. Your uterus grows a fleshy lining each month and in the middle of that month, an ovary will release an egg. If that egg isn't fertilised into becoming a baby, then the lining of the uterus is unnecessary, and so it breaks down and comes away from your body, out through your vagina. It seems like blood, usually a bit thicker than your normal blood, and it needs to be absorbed.

Most girls use pads to soak up their period when they first start. You can get these in packets and they have an adhesive strip so that they can sit securely inside your undies. When you need to replace your pad, tear it off your undies, fold it over, place it in the toilet or bathroom bin, and put a fresh

pad in place. Never, ever try to flush a pad—you don't want to inflict that sort of blockage on a poor, unsuspecting plumber!

Tampons are small cylinders of wadded cotton which you insert into your vagina. They're useful if you need to swim when you have your period, and they also help to keep any smell from escaping. However, it can take a little practice to get used to using tampons, and it's a good idea to use pads for a while until you get used to how heavy or light your period is, so that you can estimate how often you should change your tampon. Like pads, tampons should never be flushed. Also, you need to have very clean hands, and never leave a tampon in for more than eight hours, or overnight, or you will risk getting toxic shock syndrome. Virgins can use tampons and using a tampon *doesn't* mean that you're no longer a virgin - that's a myth!

It's the truth that periods kind of suck, but they don't have to be the end of the world, either. If you find that you're getting really bad cramps and aches, then go for a power walk or do some other form of exercise to warm up your muscles. If you're having trouble sleeping due to cramps, then take a hot water bottle to bed—wrap it in a thin towel and hug it to your belly. A cup of tea or a hot chocolate might help too.

If, however, you find that your cramps are serious enough to make you vomit, or prevent you from standing up, then you should see your GP. It's also probably worth seeing your GP if you still haven't had your first period by the time you're 15.

If your periods are really irregular in the first year, don't worry—it takes a little while for your body to learn what to do and when! But after the first year, you should settle into a reasonable routine of having a period every four weeks. But if after the first year you feel that your period schedule is still too crazy, then book in to see your GP.

SEX.
TO DO OR NOT TO DO?
that is the question.

So, you've got a boyfriend (or a girlfriend!)—that's awesome! But what now?

Starting a relationship is about getting to know each other—things you like to do (together and alone), what you think about things, what you find funny, sad—you name it, there's so much to learn about each other and that's a really enjoyable part of any relationship.

As you get to know each other and explore each other's personalities, you'll build trust and intimacy, which often leads to sexual acts. It's totally fine to have a relationship without sex, and as you get older you may also have sex without a relationship. But when it's your first time, it's a whole other ball game. If you're considering having sex or trying sexual things with your partner, keep reading!

So, you're getting kind of close? You might find yourself sitting on the bus, or on the quad during recess, and spending time together outside of school. Depending on your personalities and a whole load of other things, you'll probably be pretty casual; hugs, hand holding, and the occasional brief kiss goodbye.

After a while you'll find you trust one another and you're more comfortable being yourselves than you were at the start of the relationship. You might find yourselves curled up together on the couch, and kissing is a normal part of your relationship. This stage might only take a few weeks—but for others it can be months or years—it really depends on the couple. But it's at this point that the question of whether or not you're heading towards sex comes up.

If your partner is older than you, you might feel like things are going too fast—if that's the case, say so! Be a strong, proud woman and don't deny what you feel. If your new partner respects you, they won't push your boundaries. And if they don't respect you, have some self respect and get out of the relationship. If they're not going to respect your feelings this early on, it will only get worse. As soon as a partner realises they can push you around, the pattern is set. Be strong. There's no shame in not wanting to have sex just yet.

How do you know when you're ready?

So, you've had some steamy moments with your partner, but you haven't had sex yet, and you don't know if you're ready. That's okay! Everyone has to make this decision in their lives. Ask yourself these questions to help you work it out.

Do I want to have sex? If the simple, honest answer to this is no, then say so! If you force yourself into it now, you will only regret it later, and

that's a horrible feeling to live with.
If the answer is yes, keep reading to make sure you're prepared.

Do I have contraception, or will I get some soon? If you're not already on the pill, or don't have some condoms in your drawer, or have some other form of contraception, then you need to get your hands on some before things go any further. A good rule of thumb is if you're not responsible enough to call the doctor or visit a chemist and get some contraception, then you're not ready to have sex. Imagine what it would be like to tell your parents you want to go on the pill; okay, now picture telling them you caught an STI or you're pregnant. See why it's so important now? Go for the far less awkward talk!

I'm 14, but I feel I'm ready. You may feel ready now, but you want to be certain; don't leave even a chance that you could look back and regret your decision. There's a reason there are laws regarding underage sex. The laws vary from state to state across Australia, but it's best to stick with them—they're a good guideline.

Is s/he the one I want to sleep with? In short, you can never be 100% sure, but if your partner is pushing you, then they're probably not the one. If they're letting you take your time, being considerate about your feelings, and discussing things like contraception with you, then you're more likely to be able to relax and enjoy this next step in your relationship. Listen to your instincts—if it feels wrong, then it probably is.

The risks of sex

1. You can't get your virginity back—once it's gone, it's gone!
2. If you're under 16—which makes it illegal in Australia, and other parts of the world—and your partner is over 18, he can be charged with statutory rape, which your parents might be

inclined to do if they feel he talked you into it!

3. You're not going to keep him in a relationship by sleeping with him. No matter what you think, this never, ever works. Never has, never will. While you might be lucky enough to meet someone who is prepared to wait, there are plenty of others out there who will say anything they need to just to get you into bed—so unless you've been in a relationship with him for a while, don't fall for it!

4. You're risking STIs and pregnancy if you haven't sorted out your contraception. An STI or unplanned pregnancy will change your life and it's much less embarrassing to duck into the chemist in a disguise to get some condoms, than to walk in to get a pregnancy test or a prescription for that disease you just caught!

5. Your reputation. People like to gossip and if you don't know that you can trust him not to tell absolutely everyone about it, then hold off until you know he'll respect your privacy.

What to expect

So, you've decided you'll sleep with your partner. If you're not feeling any shame, guilt or anxiety after making this decision, then, great! Now, you have a load of tools at your disposal to make sleeping with your partner amazing.

First, learn everything you can—read books, magazines, websites and so on. While your friends might be helpful or interesting, remember not to base all your knowledge on what they say; sex is different for everyone, we all like different things, and there are plenty of urban myths related to the ups and downs of sleeping together, that listening too hard to your friends might freak you out!

Secondly, choose your contraceptive weapon! Talk to a trusted parent or older sister, or see your GP. You'll need to see your GP for most contraceptives, such as the pill or any device that needs to be

medically inserted. As well as these, you'll need a barrier contraceptive—a physical barrier like a condom or diaphragm. These are important; the pill might stop you from getting pregnant, but it doesn't protect against STIs! Be proud and protective of your health; take responsibility for your sexual health and always use a barrier method.

Know your body and your comfort zone—just because you've gone this far, doesn't mean you still don't have the right to say 'no'. If he suggests things that you feel weird about, be nice but clear that you're not interested. There's always later if you change your mind, but you can't undo regret!

Finally, try not to expect too much. Especially if he's a virgin too; neither of you are likely to get it completely right the first time! It can still be a really special experience though, if you're comfortable with each other. If you trust each other you can laugh your way through it, but it's unlikely to be earth-shattering the first time around! Just relax; you probably look gorgeous and he's so excited just to be this close to you that he's not going to judge you for anything. Don't worry about how your hair looks or if he's bored. Just enjoy the trust and closeness.

> If something seems different 'down there', such as weird bumps or itching, and there's a chance you may have an STI, see a GP immediately. Don't put it off!
>
> Also, if your period is late and you've had sex—even if you've used contraception—there is a chance you could be pregnant. Get your hands on a pregnancy test (go to an out-of-town chemist if you're worried about being spotted), and if it's positive, book yourself in with the GP. You can keep your baby, adopt it out, or have an abortion (also called a termination, ending your pregnancy); a GP can help you with all three options. Discuss each option with your parents and/or a trusted friend.

True or False?
SEX AND LOVE MYTHS EXPLAINED

'Using a tampon means I'm not a virgin'
FALSE

The only thing that will make you 'not a virgin' is if you have sex. Anyone who tells you that tampon use takes away your virginity, quite simply, is wrong!

You can use a tampon from your first period, but it's best to start with pads until you get used to how heavy your period is likely to be on certain days; this will help you estimate how often you'd need to change a tampon.

The biggest benefit of tampons is that they allow you to go swimming while you're on your period. But if you're not a swimmer, and the thought of tampons freaks you out, then that's fine! There's nothing wrong with using pads. It's all personal choice.

'If I'm pregnant, I'll feel nauseous'
NOT ALWAYS TRUE

'Morning sickness' (nausea in the mornings) is a common symptom of pregnancy—but don't rely on that alone! Even if you feel absolutely fine, you may still be pregnant. So, regardless of whether or not you're feeling ill before breakfast, if your period is late it's worth checking it out.

Go with a parent, guardian or trusted friend to a chemist or family planning clinic to get a pregnancy test. If it's negative, relax, and if you still haven't had your period in two weeks, get and take another test.

If it's positive, book yourself in with a GP. Your options for carrying the baby to term are either becoming a parent, or adopting out the baby to other parents. Alternatively, you can book in for an abortion or termination, which is where your pregnancy is ended medically or via a surgical procedure. Terminations usually have to happen early on in the pregnancy, so be sure to book in with a doctor the minute you can. It will give you maximum time to make your decision.

If you or a friend are pregnant, support is the most important thing. Make sure you, or your friend, have at least one trusted person to lean on. It's also good if you're able to discuss the problem with your parents—and if you're keeping the baby you need to talk to them about it, as it will change their lives as much as yours.

'The Pill prevents genital diseases'
FALSE

The Pill (or other contraception that uses medicine, like contraceptive implants) is a wonderful thing—if you take it regularly it will prevent pregnancy, and you can even use it to put off your period (camping trip, here I come!). But it's a medical contraception; it's not a barrier method. The Pill cannot protect you from STIs.

The difference between the two is that pregnancy is caused from sperm fertilising an egg, whereas some STIs only need skin-to-skin contact to infect you. The Pill is a great invention, but it's not magic!

If you're with a new guy, or if there's even the slightest chance the guy you're seeing may have an STI, always use a barrier method like a condom. As embarrassing as it can be to get condoms, it would be more embarrassing to have your mysterious down-there disease checked out by the doctor, right? The Pill is great for preventing pregnancy, and condoms are a good double-up to back up that protection and also prevent STIs. Take care of yourself and use both!

'Losing your virginity really hurts'

NOT ALWAYS TRUE

The part of what hurts when you lose your virginity is the breaking of a part of your body called the hymen. The hymen is a thin covering of skin and when it breaks, there may be pain and some blood, or you may not even notice!

Your hymen can actually be broken in other ways; even something as innocent as horse riding can take care of that. Even with a broken hymen, you're still a virgin if you haven't had sex—older civilisations used to see the unbroken hymen as the mark of virginity but in modern society we see that there's always a chance it's been broken through sport or other means, and has nothing to do with sex!

So, regardless of the hymen being broken or not, having sex the first time might be a little painful at first, and there may be a bit of blood; or you may feel little or no pain or discomfort. Unfortunately there's no way to predict it, but if you're really worried, just wait. Have sex later when you're comfortable and feel ready.

'I can't get pregnant before my first period'

FALSE

Sorry—you can! The problem with first periods is that they're impossible to predict, so if you're having sex and your first period is only weeks away, you can easily get pregnant.

Generally, though, if you haven't had your period yet, it's better not to have sex anyway. Periods are our body's way of ushering us into womanhood, and until your body is in that adolescent stage, you're not likely to have all the hormones and responses you need to actually *enjoy* sex! So what's the point?

If you hit 16 and you still haven't had your period, it's worth seeing a GP just to find out why not. It might be lifestyle factors or just a quirk you've inherited from your mum; perhaps late periods run in your family. But it's worth just checking with a doctor for peace of mind as much as anything; if they find something wrong, then you know and can fix it, and if nothing's wrong then you can relax!

If you've heard a rumour and you're not sure if it's true, it's always best to ask a parent, your GP, or a health teacher. While you can often find the answer on the internet, you'll also stumble across plenty of wrong answers too!

The Sexuality Question

**More and more teenagers are proudly identifying as gay.
Homosexuality is not a disease, nor is it a choice, and it's definitely not wrong.
If you think you might be gay, read on, and know you're not strange, and you're not alone!**

'What's wrong with being gay?'

Nothing. Nothing at all. It's like asking what's wrong with having brown eyes, or being able to run really fast. It's the way you were born and there's not a lot you can do about it. Well, you can choose to fight it, to pretend that you're not gay and try to live a hetero life, but apart from lying to the world around you, you will also be lying to yourself, and that's not a healthy way to live.

Think about how you would feel if your best friend told you he or she was gay. Would it change them as a person? Would you still want to be friends with them? Chances are, if they're wonderful and sweet enough to be your best friend, you wouldn't want to throw all that away just because they happen to like the same gender. So if you wouldn't cut your best friend out of your life just for being gay, why would you hate yourself for it?

All you have to be in life, to sleep at night, to get on with others, is a good, honest person. Your **sexuality** has nothing to do with whether you're a good person or not. Your **choices** are what defines you: whether or not you kick dogs for fun (bad!), or help little old ladies across the road (good!). Your sexuality is not a choice, it's part of who you are, and regardless of it, you are still a beautiful person—if you choose to be! There are loads of gay people who contribute to society, are happy and healthy, and in love. The only thing it really changes is *who* you love!

And remember: you don't ever have to give yourself a label. When you're comfortable with your preferences, you might consider adopting the label 'gay', or 'lesbian', or 'bisexual', but you could quite easily go your whole life never classing yourself, and as long as that's not causing you stress, it's fine.

Telling Your Parents

Once you feel confident that you are gay and that it's not just a passing phase, it's probably time to start 'coming out'. This can be hard—especially if your family or friends have strong anti-gay feelings—and only you can decide the best time, but once you come out, life does become easier because you're living your life as YOU, and not pretending to be someone you're not.

Generally speaking, most parents will come to terms with it, but if they didn't suspect, then you need to remember that even the best of parents can succumb to shock, so be patient.

If you're really lucky, though, then there's a good chance that you'll only be confirming what they already suspected—you'd be surprised how well some parents know their children! And if that's the case, then getting it out in the open will make everyone feel much better, much sooner.

If you're having trouble working out how to tell your parents, then maybe you need to talk about it with an older brother or sister first. They can then perhaps support you while you tell your parents.

It often helps to give clues so that they're prepared for the talk. Idly say how attractive a girl is in a magazine, and even drop stereotypical hints if you have to. A lot of parents stereotype lesbians as liking to play sport and gay guys as liking to shop—rely on that if you have to, just to get the idea into your most supportive family member's head. Set a time to talk to them where there are no distractions—book it in advance with them, even. Beforehand, practise what you're going to say. This might feel weird but it helps if you have an idea of how to answer any questions they might have. Research stories of other gay teens and how they came out, for inspiration.

Sit down with your most supportive family member somewhere private and quiet. Start the conversation with something like: 'The reason I'm telling you this is because I love that we have an honest relationship and I really want to continue that with you. But if you want me to keep telling you the truth, I need you to try and be understanding when I tell you this.' Follow it as simply as you can. Make it clear: 'I think I might be gay', 'I'm a lesbian', 'I'm pretty sure I'm bisexual'. Use direct words so that they can't misunderstand you and avoid the issue. Understand that there will probably be shock or surprise, which may manifest itself as anger. Say 'I understand that you're shocked and angry but I didn't choose this and it's been difficult/a long process for me to come to terms with. I'll give you as much time as you want but I'd really love your support. This doesn't have to be a bad thing, or a big deal.'

Never raise your voice, don't accuse them of anything, and just drill into their heads that you need them there for you. Once your most supportive family member is on board, telling the rest of your family should be much easier. It helps to learn how to joke about it, and especially learn how to be the butt of jokes about it—laughing about something is a great way to come to terms with it. Make jokes, be open about it, try not to be offended if your loved ones rely on stereotypes to try to understand your situation—at least they're making an effort!

You may need to readdress the situation in the future—for example, even if they seem totally okay with you being gay, it would help to let them know first before bringing your partner home for dinner. If they love you, they'll make an effort to be okay with your choices, but it may take a little while for them to get into the routine. And if your mum cries about never being able to have grandchildren, gently remind her that this is the 21st century and science has come a long way! With patience and an understanding of their reactions, eventually you'll be able to come to some kind of agreement and a state of acceptance. And if they really refuse to accept it or listen to you—get another adult involved to help.

Dealing with Homophobes

Unfortunately, homophobes, like racists, have always been with us and probably always will be. If you find you're being subjected to homophobic behaviour, you need to remember:

- most homophobes are acting that way because they can't be bothered understanding what being gay means
- most homophobes are basically ignorant
- most teenage homophobes aren't thinking for themselves; they're repeating what they've learnt from parents or older siblings.

You have the right to feel safe at home, at school and out in public, so if you find that you're being bullied by homophobes, seek help before it gets out of hand. Tell your friends, so that they can keep an eye out for you. Speak to a teacher, counsellor, parents or siblings. Whatever you do, don't suffer in silence! Homophobic behaviour is bullying, which is something nobody should have to endure.

Relationship Politics

In your first few relationships, you're working out what it means to be a girlfriend. Whether you're with a guy or a girl, it's still new ground and even though there shouldn't be, there are often games involved. Testing your new partner's devotion is never a good thing, but if someone's playing love games, it helps to know what the possible consequences can be.

playing hard-to-get   Danger rating: 7/10

The game: You don't return his calls, ignore him when he talks to you, and act flirty, but like you don't really care.

Why we do it: You either feel vulnerable and you're trying to gain power in the relationship, or you're trying to make him want you even more.

Best outcome: Guys often respond well to a

challenge so if you're leaving him hints that you enjoy the chase, he might respond positively and chase you. You'll eventually have to let him catch you, though!

Worst outcome: He'll get bored and move on, and you'll look like the crazy girlfriend that doesn't know how to show her love.

being super-clingy

Danger rating: 8/10

The game: You call him five times a day and cry when he doesn't return your texts. You try to spend every waking second with him.

Why we do it: You may feel like he wants to spend more time with his mates than you, or you may unconsciously be trying to annoy him to test his reactions.

Best outcome: He'll like it and mimic your behaviour—but beware, if you're not naturally clingy, his responsive clinginess might get a little annoying!

Worst outcome: He'll get angry at you for not giving him any space, and for smothering him. You might end up on a break, or just broken.

Always fighting? Something has to change!

starting fights over nothing

Danger rating: 9/10

The game: You flip out at anything he says, give him the silent treatment for days, and act way too offended at jokes.

Why we do it: You may feel like you need to punish him for something and it gets a bit addictive having the power of making him feel guilty and small.

Best outcome: He'll clue in to what you're doing and buy you flowers with a great big apology card, and you'll drop the game because you feel so guilty!

Worst outcome: He'll get mad or hurt at your incessant anger and either leave you, play your game himself or start getting all needy and pathetic.

demanding too much

Danger rating: 8/10

The game: You expect him to take you everywhere and call you all the time. You've made him quit football to come watch you dance, and he gets nothing in return.

Why we do it: You might be copying a bad example of a relationship, or you might feel that this is how he should show he cares.

Best outcome: He'll love you enough that he'll patiently serve your every request and more. Watch out, though—even the nicest boys have a limit to their patience.

Worst outcome: He'll realise he deserves to have his own life, and he'll remove himself from yours before you've even realised there's a problem.

Together forever ...

... OR NOT

You were drawing his name in hearts on your notebook, and thinking about your wedding dress and how your name would sound with his surname. It felt like love. It felt like forever. Unfortunately, he wasn't feeling the same way.

It's a brutal shock when someone you adore tells you they don't want to be with you anymore. They might even use a lame excuse like 'we never see each other' (even if you're neighbours!) which hurts even more because you're not hearing the truth. The truth hurts, too.

So, you've been dumped. The boy you thought you'd graduate high school with has decided that's not the future he wants. Why wouldn't you be angry? Unfortunately, anger will get you nowhere. Neither will dwelling on it. What you need to do is understand why it happens, and how to move on.

thereason

There's a chance his parents told him he couldn't go back to boxing class if he had a girlfriend. There's a chance he's secretly moving to Romania. There's a chance it's not about you at all, and breaking up with you was awful for him.

Unfortunately, there's an even bigger chance that he's just bored. Bored, or interested in someone else, or just wanting to be single and hang out with his mates. In primary school you didn't need a reason to break up, and even in early high school it's not so upsetting. But once you start getting older and entering into more serious relationships, especially those involving crossing frontiers (for example, if he was your first kiss), the reasons start to matter, and they start to hurt.

What you need to remember first is that it's not a rejection. He went out with you in the first place, and if you had some good times then he obviously liked you as a person. Even if he says 'you've changed', it doesn't mean you've changed for the worse. It just means that you and he aren't a good fit anymore, and that's okay. You don't have to be a good fit. People change.

And that's the thing about being a teenager. We change very quickly—it could be that when you met and started dating, you were great for each other. And you changed as you grew, and suddenly you realise you're two very different people. And as two very different people, you don't get along, or there are parts about one another that you aren't happy with.

So if that's the reason that he dumped you, you should just be glad that you're growing and changing and that he's mature enough to realise that staying together would only make you hate each other. Yes, breakups are and will always be a slap in the face, but if you look at it in this way, it's much easier to come to terms with it.

Think of it this way. You bought a dress in year 7. It suited your style, it fitted your curves, you liked the colour … then. Now you're in year 9 and it's too short, too tight around your chest and it's a little too girly for your taste now. You wouldn't keep wearing it—you'd give it away. And you might just give it away to someone who completely adores it. So how do you know that when the once-perfect boyfriend leaves you, that he's not leaving you wonderfully single for an even better guy to come along? Maybe he's doing you a brilliant favour. You'll just have to wait and see.

thereaction

It's really hard to restrain yourself from slapping someone in the face when they're standing there telling you they don't want you anymore. But that's the worst thing you can do.

If they're being awful and they deserve a serve, give it to them—verbally. Don't cry, and don't go crazy, but tell them calmly and maturely what they've done to annoy you. However, if they were a great boyfriend right up until the breakup, and they've phrased it gently and obviously feel bad, the best thing you can do is just stay calm. Smile at them, say 'That's a shame, but I'm sure I'll understand it in time'. If they ask if you're upset, be honest but not dramatic. Say 'I'm a little shocked right now, but I'll be okay.' A reaction like this can change how he feels: it'll make him feel relieved that you've been so mature and you'll be friends again sooner, or he'll realise he's making a mistake and he'll want you back within days. Either way, you refuse to be the victim and you walk away strong and empowered. And that's attractive as hell.

theremedy

It's happened, you've gotten home from school, you're safe indoors. You can cry now. Cry, call a friend and cry more, write an angry diary entry—get the emotions out.

Girls all over the world will tell you this: the best way to help any jilted girlfriend is ice cream and movies with her friends. Have a girls' night in. Buy the most decadent ice cream you can afford, rent some films—go romantic and get teary or get comedy or horror and forget the whole thing—and have your best friends over for the night. There's nothing like feeling supported, and after just one night like this you'll remember how great the single life can be.

What you deserve from a partner

'I got you the perfect Christmas present—me!'

You deserve:

To be respected
Not to be pushed into anything you don't want to do
Someone who will laugh with you
The right to say 'can we meet up tomorrow instead? I'm tired today' and not start a fight
Someone who will hear your side of the story in an argument
Someone true to themselves—if they're being what they think you want, they're not being them
Someone with their own life, and friends, who doesn't completely rely on you
To be able to trust your partner
The occasional text or phone call to let you know they love you
To feel comfortable with your partner
Dates where you do absolutely nothing, and other dates where you're spoiled rotten and get to dress up
A partner who is also a friend

Your partner deserves:

Your respect, love and patience
The knowledge that they can be themselves without you judging them
The ability to reschedule a date (with enough notice) and not start an argument
Your loyalty and trustworthiness
Space from you occasionally
Time with their friends and family
To have you listen to his/her side of the story in an argument
The freedom to make jokes and laugh with you
To feel good about themselves around you
The right to say 'no' to an invitation from you

ten top tips
about love and sex

Any guy that pressures you, or doesn't want to use contraception, is not the kind of guy worth sleeping with. Be a strong, proud woman and tell him firmly to back off. You have every right to say no until you're ready—and 'ready' depends on who the guy is, too.

A general rule for knowing if you're ready for sex: if you're too afraid to buy condoms or get a prescription for the Pill, then you're not mature enough to be having sex. Protection comes first!

Don't put off seeing a GP if your periods are accompanied by really painful cramping, vomiting or diarrhoea. There are a number of solutions for symptoms this bad, so don't just live with it! Fix it.

Don't forget—nobody can love you until you honestly love yourself. Until you respect yourself as a person and like who you are, nobody else will. Your most popular friends probably accept themselves! Try it.

Being gay is not wrong. It's not even weird. It's just different. Getting used to the idea that you or a friend might be gay can be an unfamiliar process to go through, but you owe it to yourself, or to them. Life can be easier when the truth is out!

Break-ups are sad, yes, but they're also inevitable. Sending nasty texts weeks after the event will only drag it on and make things worse. It's healthiest to accept the new direction, and stay positive.

Before you start a fight over something with your partner, switch places in your head. If it was you who forgot to call, would he be mad at you? Would you even feel like you'd done something wrong? Act accordingly.

Your parents, friends and partner might want you to keep a baby or have an abortion, but remember that the final decision is completely up to you. It's your body and your life. Take advice, especially from professionals such as a GP or counsellor, but be firm in your choice.

Your friends can be the best thing about a break-up. Instead of feeling sad about the split, focus on how much more time you have for your friends—and for fun!—now that you're single. Make the most of your situation.

You and your friends will all go through big changes in relationships and sexuality during high school. The most important thing is to remember that it's all normal, and if you talk to your friends you'll often find out that they're in the same situation. Stay open about it!

work
life

A collaboration with Tracy Keith

Haven't got a job? Not to worry. This chapter will help you write an impressive resume, juggle work and school, and do the best you can in a customer-oriented job, even if you feel like hiding behind the counter. It's time to start your career!

Writing a KILLER Resume

You need a resume to get a good job—but how do you write a good resume when it seems like all you've done all your life is school?!

If you've never had a job before, it can be tricky to write an impressive resume (also called a CV). You might feel like you have nothing to offer. But the important thing to remember is that you're probably more skilled than you think!

So what do you put in your resume when you have no work experience?

Focus on what makes you perfect for work! Get some paper and make a list, using the topics below as headings. By the time you're finished you'll have some really good points to list in your resume.

And remember—it might feel like bragging, but a resume's purpose is to make you look good! Set the modesty aside and start listing all the things you're proud of doing …

- **School achievements and activities:** the subjects you took and the marks you got, student councillor, sports teams, interschool competitions, school production, peer support, etc.
- **Academic achievements:** came first in the class? Write it down!
- **Voluntary work:** if you donated blood, collected

money, worked at the RSPCA—anything you did out of your own desire to help others is perfect for a resume.

> **Any one-off jobs—even babysitting, delivering papers, dog walking, lawn mowing, painting, leaflet delivery, etc.**

- **Groups you belong to:** Scouts or Guides, drama club, dwebating, sci-fi, horticulture club, and so on.
- **Computer skills:** list all the programs you can use, like Microsoft Word or Adobe Photoshop. If you're good with a program, say so! This includes using the internet and email. Write it all down.

- **Awards received:** such as Duke of Edinburgh, most improved in subject, scholarships, etc.
- **Any referees:** people who can comment on your reliability, honesty, communication skills and work ethic. These don't have to be employers—you can use religious leaders, teachers, people you have volunteered with— even your sports coach or theatre director. Make sure you get permission from your referee to list them on your resume with their details, and get an agreement from them that they'll hold up their end of the deal and talk you up if a prospective employer calls them and asks about you.

> **If you've written everything you can think of and only filled a paragraph, read on!**

Schools are actually brilliant for getting ready for work. Listen just once on assembly and you'll hear a number of clubs mentioned and opportunities offered. If you take part in just one or two of these extra-curricular opportunities, you'll develop a wealth of skills and experience that are totally worth writing on a resume. It's all about making the most of what you've got.

Maximise Every Opportunity

Look for ways you can learn new skills, meet new people, push your own boundaries—scare yourself. Try new things—even if you hated it, when it's over you'll still have learnt from it, and those skills and your experience is one more for the resume.

- Get involved in the **school production**—sing, dance, do lighting and sound, costume design, computer graphics, publicity, or sell tickets.
- Participate in **school camps**—step up and be a leader.
- Try something you've never even considered before, like **debating** or the **soccer team**
- **Assist** in the canteen, library, office or staffroom.

- Join **Duke of Edinburgh,** Scouts, or Guides.
- Voice your opinion in the **Student Representative Council.**
- **Mentor a junior student** in a subject you are good at or join a **peer support program.**

Get Good Karma

Volunteer work is one of the best methods for personal development. Give up just one Saturday for a charity door knock, and reap the benefits:

- **Learning new skills:** anything from customer service to administration.
- **Meeting new people:** go home with good karma *and* new friends!
- **Having fun:** you'll feel great about what you're doing and it can be really enjoyable.
- **Connecting with people** who could become a referee—don't forget to ask first!
- It shows **dedication, perseverance and initiative**—employers will see all these traits on your resume.
- It can **open doors to other opportunities**— keep in touch with your charity leader and you might find yourself in a paid job with the charity!

Cover Your Bases

If you've never written a resume before, it can be daunting to work out what to write and how to write it. Language must be professional but the passage should still flow, and try not to use 'I' at the beginning of every sentence as it can get exhausting for the reader. Too much to remember, right? Ask a teacher to read it over, and then ask a parent or guardian. Get as many adults as possible to make suggestions, because each one will probably think of something else. Get someone to edit it—nothing is worse than a resume full of typing errors! Lay it out however you want but make sure each section is clear and relevant.

Formatting

Most resumes use strong headings and are set out using bullet lists and tables. Tables are really useful for setting out information such as your education history, which can often look quite messy if written straight out. Format the table to have invisible borders and your resume will look even neater.

If you can afford to get your resume printed in colour, a splash of consistent colour (pastels and darker colours like navy blue are most professional—avoid neon!) can really make your resume stand out. If black and white printing is your cheapest option, print it on cream or pastel paper to make it eye-catching. Print double-sided where possible.

Resume Headings

You don't need to include all of the following headings—leave a heading out if you have nothing to write underneath it, or meld two headings into one if your answers look really short.

NAME: Pretty obvious, this one! Your name should be a title across the top of the page, big and bold. 'Resume of Julia North', 'CV—Julia North' and 'Julia North—CV' or even just 'Julia North' are all appropriate headings.

DETAILS: Your address, phone number and email address should all be included in the resume. You could put your name in a small, pale font on one side of the header and your phone number on the other, and/or include all your details at the beginning of the resume. If you're going for a job in media such as photography, modelling or journalism, a link to your blog or online portfolio is a nice touch.

CAREER OBJECTIVES/MOTIVATION: Your hopes and dreams! Here you want to be writing something like, 'I really love animals and would like to work in an environment where I can care for them. I am studying science at high school and plan to study vet science at university next year, and eventually own my own veterinary practice.' A sentence or two of this length will suffice. Be honest if you have a few dreams—for example, 'I aspire to experience working a number of roles in show business—my skills and interests range from publicity to performance.'

EMPLOYMENT SUMMARY: If you have nothing in this section, go and do some voluntary work. It's important to have something here to show that you've sought out opportunities! Set out jobs (casual, one-off, work experience and voluntary) by year, with the most recent at the top. It's best to do this in a table: the first column with the month and year you started and finished each job, the second column lists the company and the third will list your role. Alternatively you can do this in two columns with the company as a header—just make sure the formatting is consistent and clear.

EMPLOYMENT HISTORY: List your major achievements and duties in each of your prior roles at work. Try to limit this to a page if possible—list only the best achievements or most interesting duties.

EDUCATION: Yep—school finally pays off! Again, in a table is best, ordered by year with the most recent at the top. Primary school isn't always necessary but if you went to, say, a performing arts school or a sport school, leave it in. Include your highest qualification (if you're Australian, that'd be the School Certificate or HSC unless you left beforehand) and also include the subjects you took and your marks.

PERSONAL ACCOMPLISHMENTS: This is where all that extra-curricular stuff comes in handy! Anything you did here that you're proud of, put it in. For example, if you were a prefect in primary or high school, or in the dance troupe, did something for charity or managed the sport team. Out of school things like Scouts or knowledge of another language can go here, too.

COMPUTER AND EQUIPMENT SKILLS: This is more and more important in modern-day society. If you can use Microsoft Word, Excel, Adobe Photoshop, EFTPOS or coffee machines, or equipment that the job you're applying for might use, say so. Any experience is worth listing, and you can separate them into 'Confident with:' and 'Learning:' to show which things you're better at.

TRAINING AND DEVELOPMENT: Courses, courses, courses. If you have a barista certificate, first aid certificate, or if you've done a computer or retail course—any learning in course form or class form outside of school can go here.

INTERESTS: These are optional, of course, but if they're relevant to the job you're going for they're worth putting in. If photography is your passion, write it down. If you really love caring for animals, put it in. Anything that will make it clearer that you'd enjoy your job is good here—keep it honest though!

REFEREES: These are especially important when you haven't been hired before. A teacher or neighbour will do if you don't have a boss to use. Ask them first if they'd be happy to be referees for you. What this means is that if an employer calls them, they'll talk about what you're like in the workplace and how good you are at this or that—so pick someone who knows how to chat! On the resume, write their name, how you know them (as in boss, neighbour, etc), their phone number, and email address. Two or three referees are enough.

Over the page is a sample of the first page of a resume. Yours might look nothing like this, but it will give you an idea of how to lay out each item, headings you might use, and the order you might have it in. Mess around with fonts and sizes until you have a resume that shows who you are and what you're about. Good luck!

JULIA NORTH - RESUME

12 Smith Street, Myville, NSW, 4998

0400 000 000   julianorth@mymail.com

Use a serious email address. It's not a good look to put 'i_love_puppies@ mymail.com' on a resume!

Career Objective

I've had a love for fashion all my life and aspire to a role in design or production of clothing or swimwear. In the meantime I'm committed to learning all I can about fashion-based retail.

Formal Education

November 2009		School Certificate	Westville Arts School
	Marks:	Advanced English	82
		Maths	78
		Science	80
		Art	93
		History	70
1999 - 2005		Primary School	Westville Selective

Skills

Languages	Italian, sign language
Computer Skills	All Microsoft Office products except Access Adobe Photoshop
Typing rate	25 words/minute
Certificates	First Aid certificate through John's Training, 2008

(search 'typing test' online to find out yours)

Employment Summary

Work Experience May 2009	Bristle Tailors, Eastville Mall *Alteration assistant and counter service*
May 2008 - March 2009	Mr Baker's Pie Shop, Westville *Counter service*

Personal Achievements/Work Related Experience

- First in Art, 2009 and 2008
- First in English, 2008
- Selected to design the poster for the school play, 2008
- Debating team, 2005 - 2007
- School Captain of Westville Selective, 2005

Julia North 0400 000 000

This resume is just an example. Your headings, layout, etc might be different, and of course this particular CV will continue over the page. Be creative with yours!

FINDING WORK

The resume is ready, and you're getting sick of being broke. You know you'd be a good employee—all you need to know is where to look for work!

You don't even have to have a boss. Take a look at the areas and ideas listed below and circle anything you think you'd be good at. Then, hit the internet for vacancies or ideas.

Service station	Assisting older people with computer use	Your parents' work
Video store	Recreation centre	Painting fences
Cleaning	Large organisations	Call centres
Ironing	Teaching music	Kitchen hand
Paper delivery	Gardening	Delivering flyers
Tutoring	Pet minding	Typing emails for older people
Babysitting	Supermarket	Restaurants, cafes
Data entry and computer work for small businesses	Lawn mowing	Dog walking
Golf course	Swimming pool	Washing cars
Takeaway	Selling art or craft items at markets	Shopping centres
Photography	Supermarket	Referee sports matches
Dance class	Retail	Deliver pizza
Movie theatre	Real estate agency	Gym
Hospital, rest home		Create your own business
		Stadium/sports ground

tracy says

"It is possible to get a job you really want and get paid for it after doing enough voluntary work. I was a volunteer helping with local events every summer, like the Teddy Bears' Picnic, Music in the Park, Chinese Lantern Festival and Special Olympics. This experience led to me getting a paid events job with the America's Cup. I have also been an unpaid extra in a music video for an up and coming New Zealand pop band. Not paid, but lots of fun!"

Applying for a job

So you've found a job you want to do. You feel you'd be good at it, and you meet most or all of the criteria. An impressive application can go a long way towards getting what you want. Tracy's compiled a list of the important things to remember when going for a job.

resume. The employer wants to see if you can be bothered creating a document to sell yourself. They want to know if you can communicate in writing. It also has all your contact details on it.

- Be prepared; bring copies of all your **certificates, awards and references** with you.
- There may be a **formal interview,** where they ask you to come and meet them in the office. You may be meeting with two or three people, or maybe just one.
- Or they may just hire you on the spot!
- The employer may want to speak to a **'referee'**—someone who knows you and can talk about your reliability, honesty, communication skills and ability to get on with other people.

what to expect

- Know that you could be **one of many people** who apply for the job you want.
- Larger organisations have processes in place that say they have to get a resume from you for their records. Don't be offended by this.
- Some organisations will ask you to **complete an application form** instead of providing a resume; others will ask you to do both.
- Even if you have no work experience and you tell them this, don't get annoyed when they say they still want to see a

Remember: you may not get the job. And you can say no thank you if the job isn't what you thought it was. For example – if they said fashion modeling and once you got there they wanted to photograph you in a swimsuit and you were not comfortable with this. Or if it requires you to travel home late at night and you do not have a driver's licence or transport. **If you don't feel comfortable or there's been a misunderstanding, just say so.** Most employers will be understanding, and those that aren't would probably be terrible to work under anyway!

the application form

A lot of larger organisations will ask you to fill in an application form for a job. Honestly, it's not as terrifying as it sounds! If you read carefully and write well, you'll impress them with barely an effort.

Most application forms will ask questions in the form of criteria. Generally, a job ad will have two types of criteria: essential, and desirable. If you meet all of the essential criteria you'll probably be pretty good for the job. It's not vital to meet all of the desirable criteria—and you may still be hired without meeting all the essentials!—just as long as you can show that you're at least part way there to being great for the job.

Read the application form carefully. Read through it first before writing anything down, and plan your answers. When a form is set out into essentials and desirables, the questions might not even look like questions—but you need to address each part as clearly as possible regardless.

If one of the criteria says something like 'Excellent communication skills', do NOT answer it with 'Yes'! Pretend you're at school and you're doing an assignment. Each answer should include the question and try to write at least two sentences where practical.

For example:

ESSENTIAL CRITERIA
Excellent communication skills
I feel I have developed strong speaking and listening skills through my time on the school debating team. I would be well suited to a job communicating with clients because I am friendly and well presented, a good listener, and I am not afraid to ask questions where I am unsure.

You might go on if you have more to say, but an answer along those lines says three key things to any employer:

You understood the question and answered it in full.
You have proof of communication skills (debating) as opposed to just claiming that you're good.
You understand several components of good communication (listening, asking questions, speaking well).

If you don't fill a particular criteria, don't just write 'No'—explain how you're halfway there or learning.

For example:

ESSENTIAL CRITERIA
Experience with Microsoft Excel
I have never used Microsoft Excel before but I would like to learn. My extensive experience with Microsoft Word means the Excel user interface is not unfamiliar, I understand the concept behind the program, and I am a fast learner. I would be willing to take a course in this program if necessary.

It's easy to put a good spin on whatever you're asked. Just think before you write and make sure your language is formal while still being readable. No point using big words if you're using them badly, but feel free to show a wide vocabulary! If it helps, pretend you're writing the application for someone else. It's easier to brag when it's not you.

THE JOB INTERVIEW

Congratulations! If you've made it past the application stage and you've got an interview, then you've already achieved something pretty great. Don't sweat it—you've got Tracy on your side.

Job interviews can be scary, but just remember that the people interviewing you are just that: people. They're not trying to make you feel awful, they just want to find the best person for the job. And while they're interviewing you, you're also interviewing them! Do you like the idea of the job? Is your potential boss nice? Are the job conditions acceptable?

When you get an interview, immediately write the details down or put them in your phone. Address, time, name of company, name of person to ask for, how many people will be at the interview—all the information you are given, write it down.

- Google the company. Nothing's more awkward than coming to an interview with no idea of what the company does, or what job you'd be doing! Do your research.
- Have a clean and tidy appearance—your school uniform is okay if you don't have suitable clothes.
- Arrive 5 minutes early and be polite to the receptionist, as they are often part of the interview process.
- Throw out your chewing gum!
- Take off your sunglasses—don't leave them on top of your head, it's very unprofessional.

- Switch your mobile phone off as soon as you arrive, or put it on silent. Don't text or call while you're waiting for the interview. Sit quietly or read a magazine.
- It's alright to ask for a glass of water. If you're asked a question and you need time to think, take a sip to buy time.
- Shake the interviewer's hand and introduce yourself—they know who you are, but it's just good manners!
- Sit up straight and make eye contact throughout the interview.
- Try to relax, smile and be polite.
- It's okay to tell them you are feeling nervous!
- Talk to the person interviewing you as you would your grandparents. Treat them with respect, and no swearing or rude comments.
- Ask them what the process is from here—will they call you? When? Should you call them?
- Thank them for their time and shake their hand before you leave. Use a line like 'I really appreciate this opportunity, this has been a great experience for me' to show them you're serious about learning and working.
- Be careful when you talk about it online! Even if one of the interviewers was a total creep, do NOT post that online. Ever. You don't know who will see your posts, or who's related to whom!

Confidence
AT WORK

Smile, honey! You're being paid to make the customers happy. If you find yourself in a customer service job and you'd rather hide under the counter for three hours, here's how to break the spell.

It can be really threatening to have to serve customers in your first few days at work. You have to understand their orders and smile, all the while trying to remember how the cash register works and where that particular book or this log is kept. Too hard! Here are some fool-proof ways to get your confidence up at work.

Fake It

You might be feeling like you want to cry, but pretend you're acting. Smile, stand tall, and when a customer approaches you, greet them with a friendly attitude and a cheerful greeting like 'Hi! How can I help you?' Be a little over the top. If you greet someone like you normally would, behind a counter this can actually look sullen. So you need to push it to 110%. It can be exhausting, but pretend you're a cartoon version of yourself. Stretch that smile a little bit wider and speak in a brighter tone. You'll be surprised how many customers absolutely love it, and it gets easier over time.

Be Realistic

Your customers are people, and all they want is to know what's going on. Don't make up things if you're not sure of an answer—it's perfectly okay to say 'I'm sorry, I'm not sure, I'll ask the manager for you' (even if you've worked there for years!). No employee is going to know everything about the job and it's okay to ask questions. Remember—it's better to ask questions, even if you annoy your boss a little, rather than make an assumption and stuff something up—especially if that means you annoy a customer! However, your boss may get annoyed if you keep asking the same questions over and over, so do try to learn and remember the answers!

Change Your Character

If you're just 'not the type' to smile and make cheesy jokes, then you need to play a character. What's this girl at your workplace like? She's chatty, she likes to laugh, and she takes care of her regular clients. Go so far as to give her a name, or a jacket or piece of jewellery that you only wear to work, to get you into character. If you're feeling under pressure or stressed, just remember that while you might be stressed, the stress stays behind at work with your character while you go home, back to your happy self!

Everyone gets a little stressed in their jobs sometimes. It's more than fine to take a few deep breaths and apologise to the customer, just say you're having a bad day. Nothing wrong with being honest! Deep breaths, keep moving.

What you deserve at work

Your Rights

You have the right to:
- ask a question when you don't understand something
- tell the customers that you're new and you'll check with the manager
- a lunch break during shifts that are legally long enough (depends on the country)
- payment that is equal to or above the minimum wage for your job and age in your country
- payment that is prompt and legal
- refuse if you are asked to do something unethical or illegal in your job
- ask for clarification of your job duties and responsibilities
- suggest improvements on systems—if you go through the appropriate channels (e.g. if there's a suggestion box, use it instead of barging into your boss's office with a report!)
- quit at any time (depending on your contract) with enough notice.

Your Responsibilities

Your responsibilities include:
- completing any task set for you by the manager to the best of your ability (excluding tasks that are unethical, illegal or involve sexual acts—see a trusted adult or even the police if you are asked to do anything sexual, immoral or illegal!)
- showing up to work on time and well-presented (if you have a uniform, wear it! Make sure it's clean and ironed)
- making every attempt to be pleasant and positive at work
- making an effort to learn your roles and the systems at work (not everyone learns quickly and it's okay to ask questions, but try to remember the answers!)
- ensuring you have transport to and from work organised before each shift
- ensuring you call up sick or busy early enough for managers to find someone to cover for you, and take as little time off as possible
- being trustworthy and following the law at work
- representing the company properly. You are the face of the business, so be what the business is: honest, efficient and caring!

ten toptips about work

1 Volunteer work is a great way to get experience and skills for your resume. Run a charity raffle, do a door knock or help with kids or the elderly. Check out your local community centre for options.

2 Print your resume on coloured paper or attach a photograph of yourself to make your resume memorable and eye-catching.

3 Check the Positions Vacant in your local paper every week for job vacancies. Look around your neighbourhood for Positions Vacant signs in windows.

4 When applying in person, make sure to ask for the manager, and then introduce yourself and explain that you are looking for a job. Ask if you can leave your resume there and be sure to thank them and smile!

5 Remove these items before going in for a job interview: gum, sunglasses, punk bracelets, heavy eyeliner, cigarettes (remove those permanently!), and your earphones!

6 A smile goes a long way in customer service positions. You'll probably have to laugh at a lot of lame jokes, too!

7 Remember, you are within your rights to refuse to perform sexual acts or illegal tasks. Talk to a trusted adult or report it to the police if this happens.

8 If your spelling isn't great, get someone to proofread your resume before you print it. Bad spelling leaves a bad impression!

9 If experience in something is required for a job and you do not have it, be honest, but also add that you are willing to learn and willing to take a suitable course. Better yet, enrol in the course and say you have signed up! Managers love proactive people.

10 If you are offered a job but by then you've realised you don't really want it, it's okay to say 'no thanks'. You don't even have to give a reason; you are within your rights to say no!

inner life

Being healthy in yourself is vital for surviving high school. Your mind, your body, even spiritually; if you don't take care of yourself you'll find final exams and social stuff a lot harder. Here's the run down on self-confidence, keeping calm, and being healthy all over.

Being
who you are

There's one thing in life that every teenager forgets. And yet, it's so important that we remember and live by this idea: it's okay to be yourself. Society sends a lot of mixed signals, but when you cut back the lies and the propaganda, you'll find that nobody really minds if you're not exactly what the magazines say you should be. It's so much more appealing to be happy with yourself.

In the spirit of that, girls from all over the world have been breaking down some of society's greatest stereotypes and double-standards. It's a revolution. It's the beginning of companies marketing real beauty, friendships being formed based on personality, and the previous ideas of popularity and success being questioned. The sooner we all get on board, the closer we'll come to knowing—and being!—who we truly are.

Learning who you are can be the hardest part of growing up. We're told we have to be confident, thin, with shiny teeth and great marks in school. We have to be academic, good at sport, and have a creative talent too. It gets exhausting! It gets to the point where we're not sure where the line is between what we are, and what we think we should be. It gets to the point where we don't know ourselves anymore.

Strip away all you want to be, and focus on what you are. Don't be mean to yourself. You might not be *athletic*, but you could be *graceful*. If you're not *musical*, are you *artistic*? And the important stuff: you might not be *confident*, but you're *trustworthy*. You might be *ethical* but not *friendly*. It's not bad, or wrong; it just is.

Once you know what and who you are, it becomes a lot easier to stay true to those concepts. Remember, though, that as you grow, what you are will change, and that's okay too. The important thing is to learn how to know yourself—know what you like, what you don't, how you react to things, and how you've changed over the years. When you know yourself, you can be yourself, and people will love you for that. Anyone who can stand up and say 'This is who I am, and I'm happy with that', is a healthy, strong person.

It does come naturally to some people—knowing and loving themselves—but for others it might take some work. Just forgive yourself if you do something out of character, and learn the lesson from it—if you reacted in a way you didn't think you would, think about that. You've just learnt something new about yourself; what sets you off, or what you do or don't enjoy. If you don't like it, then work on it! There's nothing wrong with trying to be the best person you can.

If you know somebody who always moulds to what they think other people want from them, you'll know how annoying it is. It makes you unreliable. If you're swearing you hate tomato juice one day and you're drinking it the next, people will think they can't trust you, when really all you're trying to do is get them to like you. But the best way to make friends, is to show them how awesome you truly are—with no pretending.

Just remember—you're still growing, still changing, and still learning who you are. You're not going to be perfect all the time! And how boring would that be, anyway? Much better to make mistakes you can laugh about later, and live your life the interesting way. Knowing who you are means you never have to be embarrassed at yourself, or offended by anybody else's opinions. If you are who you are, nobody can touch you.

It's completely okay to be you—imperfect, crazy, unpredictable, complete, flawed, unique, amazing, beautiful you. The more you believe that, the happier life will be.

Forgive Yourself

Relax! It's completely fine to …
- weigh more (even much more!) than 40kgs
- be shorter than 170cm
- have disobedient or frizzy hair
- not hate yourself
- settle for less
- be too lazy to go to a party
- have braces
- say something stupid and wish you hadn't
- be a bit dorky
- never get straight As
- be happy with a 56% mark
- sleep instead of partying
- wear last season's fashion
- be smart
- like computer games
- hate high heeled shoes
- not like the 'hottest' celebrity or 'best' new movie
- not want to date anybody
- have pimples
- come to school with bed hair
- wear a 10A bra
- wear a 14DD bra
- eat whatever you want
- skip the exercise occasionally
- be really tall and skinny
- look in the mirror and think 'I look pretty good today!'
- skip the 4-hour makeup routine
- own $3 cleanser
- laugh like a hyena
- not have any piercings
- wear glasses
- be a virgin
- **be happy with who you are!**

Spirituality and religion

A lot of teenagers join a religion, or leave one, during high school. It's a period of great change and it's only logical that you might need something to help you make sense of it. There are so many types of belief systems in the world and you don't even need to adopt an existing religion—you can build your own system of beliefs out of lots of different theories. Or you can choose for religion not to be a part of your life at all.

The important thing to remember about religion is that it's a matter of choice. A lot of religious institutions will tell you that those who don't believe your religion are doomed, or cursed, and you can 'save' others by helping convert them. If you really think about this idea for a bit, you'll realise it doesn't make much sense. The problem is that religion used to be pure, and it's since been corrupted with marketing campaigns and control tactics. You need to strip away the need to convert others, and be sure in your own beliefs. If you completely believe it, why does it matter if your best friend doesn't? **People who are completely invested in their own beliefs do not feel the need to convince others.**

Secondly, while some religious institutions are more powerful than others, no religion is 'wrong'. If you're a Christian, you can still get along with Pagans, even though these two religions have had a history of conflict. What we believe or where we're from does not make us better or worse people. And inside—in spirit—we're all the same.

In a way, all religions exist for the same reasons—just like people. They're all a way of understanding what's around us, why we're on the earth, and what controls our lives. Some religions have given their god a name and a picture to make the concept easier to grasp. Others consider their gods more like energies than people, and that's just another way of personifying the concept of the 'greater power'. From astrology to Scientology, religion is simply a method of learning and enlightenment—and if we won't know the truth for sure until we die, why bother wasting our lives arguing about it or forcing it on others?

People of lesser religions, unfortunately, are often the victim of misinformation. We're often told horrible things about other religions. Most of these are stereotypes, and generalisations, and they're often incorrect. It's a form of bullying, and it's a form of discrimination—it's called religionism. Treating somebody differently because of what they do or do not believe is denying them a basic human right—the right to freedom of religion.

Having a religion might help you as a teenager, or having none at all could benefit you just the same. You have to do what works for you. That could mean leaving your family religion, even just for a while, or it could mean joining a religious group or practising a religion on your own. You might even work out your own belief system. However you choose to look at life, just remember that nobody has the right to judge you for your beliefs, so long as you're not hurting anybody.

Spirituality is personal and a solid belief system, and whether drawn from an existing religion or pieced together from your own beliefs and experiences, can be a powerful mode of support during your high school years. It's whatever gets you through the night.

6 Steps to
24/7 HAPPINESS

It's possible—you can be happy all the time! Okay, maybe not literally every minute of every day, but if you follow these tips, you can get damn good at having a smile on your face!

1. DON'T TAKE IT PERSONALLY

Your friend just made a joke at your expense. Everyone's laughing but you feel like crying.

Instead of interpreting it as an insult and making everyone awkward by getting angry, see it for what it is—a joke! If your friends had any real problem with you, you'd know for sure.

And besides, even if someone is insulting you, they're not insulting you—they're insulting their view of you, which might not be what you're really like at all! We all have our opinions and what someone thinks of you might not be what you are. If you refuse to be offended, nobody can hurt you.

2. KNOW WHAT MAKES YOU SMILE

Too easy, this one. Find out when you're happiest, and make that a common occurrence in your life!

Whether it's your favourite TV show, shopping with your friends or walking your dog, do whatever makes you happy, whenever you can. Make time for happiness and it will come!

3. DON'T THINK—JUST DO

Study, asking him out, bungee jumping; anything attached to dread, procrastination or adrenaline are moments where you should just go for it!

Especially if it's something you're dreading—just think how good you'll feel once it's done, and get it done now. You'll be so relieved afterwards. Don't waste your energy on nerves!

4. LEARN THE VALUE OF WORK

Get out in the garden with your grandpa or scrub the floors. In our high-tech generation we don't move much, so we don't get that natural endorphin release. Get some exercise for a happiness boost!

On top of that, the pride you'll feel when your hard task is finished is a huge boost. Go on, grab a mop!

5. MAKE SOMEBODY ELSE HAPPY

Whether it's as big as charity work or as small as waving at your elderly neighbour, nice gestures make a huge difference.

Try complimenting a friend (make it genuine), or doing your chores before your parents ask you to. Their appreciation is your reward! You'll feel great for helping them, and they'll appreciate you even more.

6. BE YOUR OWN BEST FRIEND

You are an amazing person. You are unique, beautiful and interesting. Why is it that you can say that to a friend and really mean it, but if she says it to you you'd disagree?

Next time someone compliments you, say thank you and leave it there. Then think about the compliment. Even if you don't agree, that's their opinion of you, and that counts for something great! Learn to believe the nice things people say. If you were your own best friend, what would you say about yourself? It's really important to love who you are, so learn how to see your good traits!

Keeping Sane at High School

High school does get stressful, that's a given. Some students deal with it better than others. But there's probably one girl at your school who breezes through with a smile on her face and never seems to panic. Guess what? You can be that girl, too.

The difference between people who cope and people who don't, is that people who cope are strong enough to say 'Okay, I've had a freak-out, now's the time to focus and get through the rest of this as calmly as possible'. And anyone can do that!

deepbreaths

Breathe in … breathe out ...

Whenever you feel like it's just too much—you might have three assignments due in on the same day, or you've suddenly realised that final exams are closer than you thought—there's a really simple trick you can do to calm yourself down and avoid panicking. The thing about panicking is that you're just going to end up wasting time. What you need to be able to do in high school is accept the situation as soon as possible, to give yourself maximum time to get

through it! If you spend four days panicking and barely touching those six assignments, you'll freak out even more when you realise how late you left it. What you need is to develop your own little tricks for taking control of the situation as soon as possible.

Try these small but effective ways of calming down quickly:

1. Take deep, slow breaths. In through the nose, out through the mouth. Close your eyes if it helps, and concentrate on your breathing—

count your breaths and make sure you inhale and exhale at least five times each.

2. Sit down, lie down, stand up, go for a walk. Change your physical position, and your perspective will change too.

3. Get the blood pumping. Bash the hell out of your drum kit, go for a jog, dance furiously for a couple of minutes. Even just star jumps in your bedroom will help clear your head and get you focused on the big picture again.

4. Think to yourself, 'I'm capable of this. I have enough time/intelligence/skill to complete this task, and there are other people in my situation who may not be as lucky as me.'

5. Try to get some perspective. Avoid thoughts like 'Why does this happen to me?' because chances are there are at least six other students in your situation. Instead, concentrate on the challenge, and how you can best overcome it.

getorganised

So you're calm now—time to get determined.

Once you've calmed yourself down and can clearly see the task at hand, it becomes much easier to get organised. The best thing to do is to set a task list, and then just chip away at it.

For example, your task list might be:

Physics homework
English assignment
Monologue for Drama
Computer Studies assignment—all due Wednesday, 14 days away.

Okay, so you've got two weeks to do two assignments, learn a monologue and do some homework. Split it up into tasks—e.g. find a monologue, prelim research for Computer Studies, draft for English, Section 1 of Physics homework.

Make sure your tasks are a decent size ('write a title' doesn't count!) but small enough to be achievable ('write 2,000 words' is a bit much for one night). Put them up on a list with tick boxes—the satisfaction of ticking off a task is partly what will keep you motivated.

Then, get to it! Try to do as much as you can earlier on to avoid too many late nights at the computer. If there are tasks you can do on the bus, in the shower, over breakfast (like reading over your monologue or editing your first draft), do it. Save yourself time by working in front of the TV with your afternoon tea. Multi-task. But most importantly, just remember that you're capable. Once you're sure that you have enough time on your hands, and you're capable of completing your tasks, you'll suddenly feel much more energetic and in control. You *are* in control! And you *are* capable. Just keep those thoughts in your head as you work.

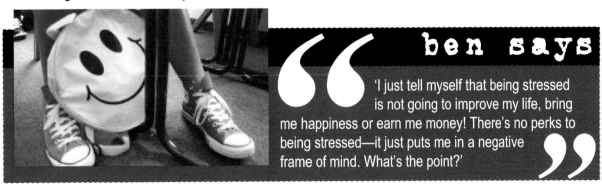

ben says

'I just tell myself that being stressed is not going to improve my life, bring me happiness or earn me money! There's no perks to being stressed—it just puts me in a negative frame of mind. What's the point?'

WHY HONESTY IS

Freedom

When you've done something wrong, the initial reaction is to lie about it. You probably want to avoid punishment. Similar to when a little white lie becomes an all-out fantasy life—but lying is exhausting and nearly always comes apart.

Here's the key to happiness: nine times out of ten, people would be more angry about the fact that you lied to them, than that you stuffed up in the first place. So if you can get into the habit of squaring your shoulders and saying 'Yep, that was me, I'm sorry'—suddenly life's a whole lot easier. Read on to find out why, and how.

'Sorry, I made a mistake'

I hear your terror, don't worry! We're brought up to think we should never make mistakes, and so when we do, our initial reaction is to pretend that we didn't. We blame it on someone else, we lie about it even being us. It's a natural reaction, but there's a better way.

Say you ate a piece of the cake in the fridge. Then your sister comes home and says 'Who ate the cake I made for my friend?' You think 'Oh, crap, I thought that cake was for us!'—honest mistake, but naturally you don't want her to be mad at you.

You could say it wasn't you, but when nobody in the family has owned up to it and you were the only one home all day, she'll find out eventually and shout at you for lying AND for eating the cake.

Or you could say 'Why the hell didn't you put a note on it?' and try to make it her fault—again, argument. She shouldn't have to put a note on a cake if she trusts her family.

So, you say 'Oh, sorry, that was me! I thought it was a cake for the family. Can I help you make another one? Maybe there's a way to piece it together so it looks whole?'

Your immediate honesty and offer to help will do three things—firstly, it will defuse the situation. She knows that it was you, she knows why you made the mistake, and she knows it was a mistake. Secondly, if your tone is calm and casual, it will help her realise it's not such a big deal, and all is not lost. Thirdly, your offer of help will make it all the harder to be mad at you, you'll probably have fun baking another cake, and all will be forgotten!

Compare that to the reaction you could have gotten if you lied or tried to blame her, and you can see why it's better for everyone to 'fess up. It's very hard for someone to keep shouting when you stand there saying 'Yeah, you're right, I did the wrong thing and I'm sorry'.

'I have no idea what that means!'

It doesn't just apply to when you're in the wrong. Even in everyday situations, if you're honest, you're free. Say you're in a conversation where you have no idea what your friends are talking about but you want to look cool, you'll probably be nodding along and laughing, but if someone asks you for your opinion, you're screwed.

What's the big deal if you didn't watch last night's episode of that terrible soap? Does it really make you a loser? No! Just say so—straight out. You won't look like a loser because you're confident enough to be honest. Just laugh and say 'Oh no, I missed it! Catch me up, what happened last night?'

It's a similar situation with not knowing a word. If you just laugh and say 'What does that mean?!', you might even find other people in the circle who were wondering, but afraid to ask. Nobody will ridicule you for not knowing—and if they do, just laugh!

'Which lie did I tell?'

When you're in the habit of embellishing your stories it can get to the point where you can't remember what you said and didn't say. Nothing's more embarrassing than when you're talking about the (totally fake) big party you were at with your cousin on Saturday night, when your friend pipes up and says 'I thought you said you spent Saturday with your boyfriend in the city?' and another friend says 'You were on chat to me all night, actually'. The minute you gain a reputation as a liar, all your stories will come under question, and your more awesome or unlikely stories that actually were true, will be dismissed.

Stick to the facts. It's okay to embellish a little (you caught lots of fish, it's okay to say hundreds because it's clear you're not being literal) and amp up the story for laughter, but keep it true for the most part! Nobody will be able to call you out or undermine your story if you're being honest.

The Benefits of Honesty

If you are who you are and speak from the heart, nobody can touch you. Honesty eliminates gossip, makes you more trustworthy, and you'll be better at telling when other people are lying.

But most importantly, you'll never have to go back on your word or suffer the embarrassment of being caught out. If you just admit when you're wrong, ask when you don't understand something, and tell the story how it happened, it will minimise the potential in your life for embarrassment and conflict.

It's (probably) okay to lie when:

Your mum asks if she looks fat
You're planning a surprise for a friend
Your friend asks how painful your piercing was
You found a receipt for your birthday present!

the power of 'GET OVER IT'

Most girls learn this in the later years of high school. The ones that don't, sadly, are often the ones who need it most. It's all about telling yourself that it's time to move on, and guess what? It actually works.

So—you're upset. You were dumped, you got a bad grade, your ex boyfriend's going out with your best friend. You had a fight with someone. You said something stupid. Someone said something mean. There are a million reasons why you might be feeling down at school, and there are another million reasons why you should learn how to pick yourself back up again.

Sometimes, in high school, making a big drama out of something seems almost glamorous. You'll notice that the girls in the middle of a freak-out get lots of attention and are the centre of some great gossip. This may be fun at the time, but eventually you'll think 'I'm really getting sick of the drama'. That's when you're likely to be biting your tongue when your friend whinges for the fourteenth time in a row, because all you want to say is GET OVER IT!

Unfortunately, it's difficult to say that as a good friend. But you can learn the trick for yourself, and others might pick it up from you. Basically, you need to put your problems into perspective. Try asking the following questions, and be honest:

- **Is my problem a common one?** *If so, then there is probably a solution. If not, then it's a good challenge for me to find a new solution and share it with others.*
- **Am I going to worry about this in a year's time?** *If not, then why worry now? If so, maybe there's something I can do to minimise the damage.*
- **Is there anything I can do to solve or minimise this problem?** *If so, I'll do it! If not, why bother complaining?*
- **Do I have a right to keep complaining to my friends about this?** *If not, I'll stop! If so, I'll make sure I gauge their reactions—they might grow tired of it quickly.*
- **Am I entitled to be indulging in self-pity?** *If not, I know what to do. If so, perhaps seeing a counsellor could help.*
- **Am I enjoying the drama?** *If so, I need to consider whether or not it's time to take the mature approach and move on from the problem. If not, my best solution is to actively try to solve or distance myself from the issue.*

True maturity is making a conscious decision to be happy—not to let the little things get you down. Obviously there are problems that require professional help, but if there's nothing you can do about the issue, your best choice will always be just to move on. Learn the lesson the issue is teaching you, deal with any guilt or anger, put the problem in the past and leave it there. For the more obsessive of us this can be difficult, but with a conscious decision to move forward, it'll get easier every day. Soon you'll find you're not even thinking about it anymore—and you'll be happier, stronger, more mature … the benefits of moving on far outweigh the benefits of holding onto the drama and letting it poison your friendships.

keeping healthy
all over

Health isn't just about eating right and exercising. It's also about keeping mentally and emotionally strong and healthy. The best thing about this is that often, one leads to the other. If you feel good about yourself you're more likely to make healthy choices. And when you make healthy choices—you guessed it—you feel good about yourself! Here's how to get into that brilliant habit of health.

Unfortunately, getting into any sort of habit takes time and determination. You might be so bogged down with study that maintaining your health is the last thing on your mind! But if you follow some of these easy steps, being healthy will soon become second nature to you— and the benefits of that are endless.

get moving

Your first step: exercise.

Yes, I know, it's relentlessly annoying and a waste of your time. But is it really? Apart from all the obvious benefits of exercise (heart health, hot body, etc) there are some lesser-known perks of a quick workout:

- The release of endorphins means you'll feel good about yourself and have more energy.
- The mind is clearer after a bit of exercise—get the heart pumping and then fill the brain with study.
- You'll feel good about doing something so positive, it acts as a motivator for other things, such as eating healthy, or getting that assignment done!
- The discipline you'll develop from sticking to your routine can be applied to study—the same applies with the organisational skills needed to plan your workout sessions.

So, you know it's good for you (unfortunately), now how do you get started?

set goals

Decide what you want, and when you want it. It might be walking up the hill without puffing, fitting into that old pair of jeans by Christmas, or even just something as simple as flattening your belly. You're capable of all of these things; you just need to know clearly what you want.

Once you've set your main goal, break it up into little goals. 'Do 10 sit-ups without resting' could be your first one, and build them up until you can do 50!

Write your goals down. It's important to have them somewhere where you can see them, and check them off or cross them out when (not if, when!) you achieve each one.

make a plan

Time management is so important. You might be hitting the gym at 5:30am, or going to the pool at 8pm—it's up to you. Wherever you can, schedule in workouts. It's good to try for three a week, but more or less is your personal decision. Or you could schedule two gym workouts, two at home workouts and one jog around the park. Mix it up. Keep it interesting.

Once you've made your plan, print it out and stick it to your wall. Schedule it in your school diary so you don't forget. And don't let your workouts clash with your favourite TV shows, because it's obvious who'll win in that fight!

push yourself

It takes about three weeks for a routine to become routine. At first, especially if your workouts are in the early morning, you might just feel like crying. This is where it helps to do your workouts with a friend or family member—with a commitment to someone else, it makes it harder just to roll over and go back to sleep.

Make sure your workouts are convenient—don't choose a gym an hour away. If you live near a park, use it! You can even work out in your own bedroom. And don't give yourself an excuse—if it's cold or raining, find an indoor alternative. Don't just skip it!

Remember: you're never going to regret doing a workout; you'll always feel good afterwards. But you do give yourself chance to regret it if you skip the workout! Effort now and results later, or indulgence now and no results. Your call.

use rewards

When it's difficult to get motivated, remind yourself of your goals, and think about how good you'll feel if you give yourself a shove and just do it. And it feels even better when you reach your goals if you have a way to reward yourself.

For your smaller goals, decide upon a small reward, and once you reach your big goal (and you will!), reward yourself really well. But don't fall into the trap of your reward being counter-productive! For example, skipping a week of workouts for reward is a bad idea (although a day or two off is okay!). So is buying stacks of chocolate. Instead, treat yourself to a massage, a day out with a friend, or even some nice exercise clothes. Buy that CD you wanted, or go see a movie. Find a reward that won't get in the way of your final goal. Your final reward should be helpful too, such as a massage, a shopping day or some new running shoes.

make it interesting

You don't have to be running on a treadmill every day to get healthy! Try the following workout ideas to get some variety:

- cycling
- walking (take your dog out for a lap of the block)
- swimming
- gym workouts
- gym classes such as spin class or circuits
- buy some workout DVDs and get fit at home
- skipping
- yoga and Pilates
- dance
- self-defence class
- gymnastics class
- weight lifting (use a spotter!)
- team and individual sports

Being healthy isn't all about the exercise, though. Eating well and keeping mentally healthy are just as important, and they'll help you reach your exercise goals as well.

eat for health

Eating healthy. We all know it's important, but what does that even mean?

Eating healthy refers to a lot of things. It refers to eating the right foods. It also refers to eating enough, but not too much. It also considers the importance of breakfast. It points to having variety in your diet, natural ingredients, keeping it fresh … it can get a little overwhelming trying to work out what's healthy and what's not. But if you try some of these simple substitutes it can get easier:

Healthy After-School Dip

Half an avocado
One tomato
Chopped dill
Lemon juice
Grated cheese
Olive oil

Dice the tomato (careful with that knife!). Mix with a handful of cheese, mashed avocado, sprinkle dill over the top, and add a splash of lemon juice and olive oil.

Eat cold as a dip with pita bread, rice crackers or wholegrain biscuits.

Snacks: check the fat and sugar content on your muesli bar. It may look healthy, but often they use processed ingredients (check the ingredients list—if there are more numbers than words, it's not good for you!) and have a high sugar content. Instead of a muesli bar, make your own trail mix—mix some rolled oats with dried fruit and nuts. Alternatively, you could try mixing just fruit and nuts with a scatter of chocolate chips.

Healthy school snack ideas: homemade trail mix or homemade muesli bars, crackers with ham and cheese, feta cheese and red capsicum slices, a piece of fruit, salad.

Lunch: it's tempting to get a sausage roll from the canteen, yes, but you can save calories and money by making your lunch at home. And it doesn't have to be a sandwich! Try out some new ideas.

Healthy school lunch ideas: chicken Caesar salad, tuna Greek salad (see below), egg salad sandwiches, pita bread and a healthy dip, wraps and burritos, turkey, cranberry and avocado sandwiches, crackers with cheese and avocado.

After school: instead of just grabbing a packet of crisps from the cupboard, get creative. Have a poke around in the vegetable drawer and see what you can make. A simple snack that will get you right through to dinner is a Greek salad with tuna. Tip a can of tuna in freshwater into a bowl, and add a few cubes of feta cheese, some black olives, slices of red capsicum and cucumber, and drizzle balsamic vinegar over the lot. It's the perfect TV snack and you won't need to count the calories!

Healthy after school snack ideas: plain crackers with ham, cheese and tomato, a piece of fruit, celery and peanut butter, crackers with cheese and olives, berry smoothies.

Dessert: avoid the temptation to use the entire bottle of chocolate sauce on your ice cream, and try something healthy instead.

Healthy dessert ideas: strawberries or blueberries and low-fat cream, yoghurt or ice cream, homemade apple pie, a banana split, or ice cream topped with Milo.

Affirmations are one of the oldest tricks in the book. For centuries we've been using them to strengthen us, sometimes without even knowing it. Ever told yourself 'I can do this'? That's an affirmation. It's all about believing what you say, and once you do, it'll be the truth.

Try this simple affirmation exercise every morning. You can even do it while you're getting ready for school. Stand in front of the mirror, look squarely at yourself and repeat the affirmation out loud, or in your head, five times. Repeat it for longer if you want to, but don't lose the meaning of the words. Think about what you're saying, and what it means, while you're saying it. Try any of the following or make up your own:

'I am strong. I know what I want and I know how to get it.'

'I am beautiful. My personality shines out from my face.'

'I am smart. I am focused, organised and determined.'

'I am confident. What people say about me doesn't affect who I am or how I feel about myself.'

'I am kind. My friends appreciate my generosity.'

Finally, there's being mentally strong. This one can sometimes be the hardest of the lot because it's difficult to tell where you need to strengthen up!

In high school, there are certain levels of ability that you'll need to have achieved. But strengthening up mentally in certain areas can help you no end.

Logic skills will help with Maths and any Science subject. Logic will also help you schedule better, interpret and answer questions more effectively, and generally just keep you on the ball.
Improving your logic: Games such as Sudoku, crosswords and logic puzzles can be bought from most newsagencies or found in the local paper. Give them a shot and see how well you go.

Handling criticism helps endlessly in your senior years and beyond. You may need to do and re-do several drafts before your work is worth submitting. If you get personally offended every time your work's returned with suggestions, you're not going to have a good time in high school! Taking criticism improves your work and strengthens you up.
Improving your ability to handle criticism: Practise. Ask your teacher for ways you could improve, and when they tell you, see it as a good thing. It's not where you're bad, it's where you could be even better. Just keep practising your approach to criticism, and it'll get easier.

Organisation is a vital tool. Organised students make the most of their study time, get better marks, and barely ever have to panic.
Improving your organisation: Practise using a diary and writing schedules and routines. Start assignments early and get into the habit of getting your homework out of the way. Organise your study notes using sticky notes, tabs, and colour-coding. You'll get the hang of it quickly!

Stress management means that high school can be more fun than frantic. If you've learnt how to relax under pressure and make the most of your time, you can sit your final exams without even breaking a sweat.
Improving your stress management skills: Check out the page

Ask your friends how they stay focused - they might just have a perfect solution!

'Keeping Sane at High School' (page 126). Organisation will minimise your stress, and stress management will make organisation easier.

Motivation and determination are often very hard to come by in high school. When all you want to do is watch TV, it can be really difficult to kick yourself into gear with study.
Improving your motivation: Set goals for yourself and put them somewhere you'll see them often, like on the wall behind your computer. Make them visual if you want. Any time you don't feel like helping yourself out with study, look at those goals.
Also, don't forget to reward yourself. It's easier to be tough with yourself and think 'no, today is for study' when you know that tomorrow is for girls' night out. You can still have a life and be good at school, it all comes down to using your time well!

If you need more motivation—just think of how good

you'll feel once the study is over and you can curl up in front of the TV with no guilt.

Self-esteem is very important. Girls who are comfortable with who they are end up confident, happy, and strong. Girls who are continually trying to change for other people will end up desperately unhappy—and people can tell when you're not being yourself. It's very annoying to know that someone is trying to please you by changing who you are.
Improving your self-esteem: Be tough with yourself on this one. It's selfish to assume that everyone's noticing how bad your hair looks today— who really cares? Do you notice anyone else's hair? And yes, everyone says stupid things occasionally. Move past it, and don't obsess. If you act confident and happy with who you are, eventually you'll become what you're pretending to be.

Discretion involves keeping other people's secrets and not gossiping. Everyone gossips occasionally, but it's about knowing where to draw the line.
Improving your discretion: Follow the simple rule. If it was your secret, would you tell anyone? If not— don't tell someone else's!

think about it

It's about **'surfing the wave'**: you can stay on top of the wave—your schoolwork and study—all year long and land on the beach easily and barely dripping, or you can let the wave consume you and you'll get thrown to shore, covered in sand and soaked. If you stay on top of the wave—kicking yourself into gear and getting that studying done while you can—the year will be easy. If you let yourself go underwater, your year will get more and more difficult as the mountain of study you've yet to do gets bigger. **Stay on top of the wave!**

quick ways
TO
spoil yourself

Believe me—you deserve this!

You might have five minutes between that study session and dinner. You've worked hard and you need to unwind, but after dinner you've got plans for the night. The solution? Spend a few minutes on yourself, and feel spoiled and content for hours.

You don't need a half-hour massage, a kilo of chocolate or a long bath to unwind. Just try these simple methods and you'll feel fresh and new in (literally!) no time.

Invest in your outer beauty. Moisturise your legs, cleanse your face or paint your nails.

Send a nice SMS to a relative or friend. Something as simple as '(song) was on the radio and it reminded me of you!' will bring good karma your way. As long as it's a nice song!

Put on one of your favourite songs and dance! You can practise a routine, or just move to the music while you do your makeup. Choose an upbeat song for an instant energy hit.

Get the blood pumping by doing some star jumps, sit-ups or jogging on the spot. You'll feel good about getting a bit of exercise and it'll leave your mind clear for hours.

Sit or lie down, close your eyes and rub some skin-safe lavender oil into your temples. Use a circular motion. Take the oil across your forehead, down the sides of your face and over the skull just behind the tops of your ears. Breathe deeply. This is great if you have a headache, and brilliant for relaxation!

Lie on a mat or your bed and take a deep breath. Contract every muscle in your body—squeeze really tight! Curl up into a ball if it helps. Close your eyes, ball your hands into fists and curl your toes under. Hold this for at least 5 seconds and then relax completely, stretching out onto your back. Try to relax every muscle in your body right after you've crunched them. You'll feel so much more relaxed after doing this even once.

Turn off your computer and phone—take yourself off the grid. Light a candle, dim the lights and meditate, or just sit or lie there and chill out with no distractions.

the darker hours

The question gets asked too often: 'Is there something wrong with me?'

Teenage life isn't easy. We change more than we're willing to admit, and sometimes too quickly for our own liking. It's sometimes difficult not to feel all alone. It's also not unusual to wonder if what you're feeling is normal. Most importantly, you need to forgive yourself for entering darker hours every now and then. As long as you come back into happiness!

it's normal to ...

... have an absolutely hopeless crush. Even if it's on someone weird like a teacher. Crushes are normal and they teach us what we like about people. The important thing is to know when it's appropriate to act on a crush, and when to let it pass.

... look in the mirror and not recognise yourself. We change so much in our teenage years that sometimes we can't keep up with ourselves. Instead of mourning the 'you' that you've lost, get to know yourself all over again. You might like what you see eventually. It's a part of growing up.

... have feelings for somebody of the same sex. You might be gay. You might not. Who cares? You're still you. Most teenagers experience this at some point. You're not abnormal at all.

... cry for hours, for no reason at all. There are a zillion and one reasons why girls cry, and 'no reason' is still a reason. Don't worry about putting it down to hormones, PMS or stress. Our bodies need the release of tears every now and then. Just let it happen, and acknowledge when the feeling passes.

... be so incredibly sick of your family that you want to run away. Try to understand that for the most part, they mean well. Get some space if you can—a sleepover at a friend's, or even just a long walk. Spend some time with pets or outdoors to calm yourself down. Space and time alone work wonders.

... hate someone and not know why. You might just need space. Try to refrain from gossiping about them if you can—you'll only feel guilty when you go back to liking them.

... never feel sad. If you feel happy most of the time then you should be proud of yourself. It means you're grateful and you're not taking things for granted. It's important not to fall into the 'glamour' of constant misery. While it's okay to be sad, it's also okay to be happy!

TEENAGE ISSUES –
Where to Get Help

This photocopy-friendly directory is mostly specific to Australia but has included as many general recommendations as possible. Often when you or a friend are faced with an issue, it's difficult to know what to do, or where to go. This list includes some suitable first steps for problems you might encounter.

Issue	Who to Speak To
Abuse and Rape	Go to the Emergency Room, your GP or call the Rape Crisis Centre.
Acne	See your GP, a dermatologist or a natural therapist.
Access to Contraception, STI screenings	Marie Stopes International can provide contraception and STI checks/treatment without a GP referral—you could also try a family planning clinic or your GP.
Anger problems	See a GP for a referral to an anger management specialist.
Anorexia/eating disorders	See a GP for a referral to a psychologist.
Anxiety and Depression	See a GP for a referral to a psychologist or counsellor.
Bullying and cyberbullying	Talk to a trusted adult or teacher, or see the school counsellor.
Fainting/dizziness	You could be low on iron, or it might be more serious. See a GP.
Family problems	Try the Kids Helpline (in Australia)—they'll know whether or not it's a matter suitable for getting the authorities involved.
Insomnia	Sleep clinics have proven to be very helpful—see a GP for a referral. Natural therapists and hypnotists can help too.
Pregnancy	If you want to keep the baby, visit your local GP or family planning clinic. Marie Stopes International can provide abortions without a GP referral—but you need a Medicare card.
Stress	Massage therapists, natural therapists, hypnotists, psychologists and counsellors can all help with stress. Or talk to a friend—they may have found a safe solution that you could try.
Study help	Ask a teacher for help in your free periods, or book in with a tutor outside of school. Talk to your parents for support.
Weight control issues	See a GP, a nutritionist, a personal trainer or natural therapist. First see a GP to make sure it's not a glandular problem, though.
Unemployment	Try your careers advisor or an employment agency.
Unexplained weight loss	See your GP.

Things I've Learnt
since Year 6

blogpost from 13.03.2009

You never realise quite how much you've changed—or grown up, thank the stars—until you look back at yourself from quite a few years ago.

So here's me, a Year 12 student, with some of the most profound (hmm) things I've learnt about life, myself, my friends and being a teenager, since Year 6!

Some of these I learnt as early as Year 6 or as late as last week. And most of them are based on mistakes I've made, or seen others make.

No order. Just as they come to me. Ready?

It's okay to love your parents.

Being mad at friends gets tiring really fast!

Children's shows are underrated.

You'll never get over a guy without an 'ice cream and chick flicks' night with your closest girlfriends!

It's okay to not know the answer sometimes, or to be wrong.

Life's bigger than how your hair looks.

Not everybody who walks past and glances over is judging you!

It's okay to take your time with sexual things. Make sure there's trust (and at least some attraction!) before absolutely anything else happens.

Popularity is a myth.

Physical beauty is overrated.

Best friends are underrated.

Shopping, comedy TV, and sleep are always the best medicines.

Broken hearts aren't really broken, just bruised. And guess what? They mend.

It's okay to not have an opinion on everything!

It's important to look in the mirror every now and then, and remember who you are and who you want to be. Hopefully these two things will be one and the same.

It helps to brush your hair.

Evenings where you don't do anything but sit around, watch TV, paint your nails, and talk to your family ... are often the best ones.

Volume of voice doesn't equal importance of words.

Don't bother complaining about the weather, because it'll never be how you want it!

> *Being sad and self-pitying gets you attention for a while, but being happy and confident gets you friends for life.*

Before you go over to the other side, take off your glasses and see how green the grass can really be right here.

Lame bands are more fun! You don't have to follow the music crowd. Everyone has at least one (or a hundred) embarrassing songs on their iPods.

Only losers write mean things about other people on bathroom walls. Those same losers smoke at lunch, swear a lot, and try to answer back to the teachers. And they think they're cool. They're not.

It's okay to be upset every now and then, even about nothing at all. But never feel guilty about having a good day!

Some things really are better left unsaid.

You can't like everyone. In light of this, just accept that some of your friends may never be able to get along. It's not your problem, it's theirs, and they'll deal with it how they see fit.

Also, you can't hate everyone! Some people deserve a second impression =]

When a teacher's told you to do something and then they yell at you for doing it, don't say 'you told me to ...', say 'I was told to ...' or 'I was under the impression I needed to ...'. It ends the argument much faster!

Angry people aren't cool.

It's fun to be immature every now and then, in moderation; giggle at the sex jokes, but lay off the nasty gossip!

Whenever you do something you later regret, think about how you'll feel about it in a month's time. It helps to know that things get better.

Always make sure your clothes aren't inside out when you put them on.

Don't expect too much from friends, teachers or family. Nobody knows exactly what to say, every time.

Honesty is one of the most important aspects of any relationship.

Don't expect or demand your teachers to 'respect' you, when you disrupt the class and talk back to them. Respect is mutual, and you have to earn theirs.

It's better to lay off the insults. Try not to take your anger out on people when you know they're not really the

142

problem. Some rifts are very hard to mend, and you'll regret flaring up for a long time.

Try not to stress about the little things.

Think in an upper-class accent when writing essays, especially for English. It helps the sentences sound more pompous, bigger words just come to you, and overall you just sound that much smarter (or more of a show-off ... which I've come to believe are one and the same when it comes to English essays!)

Always thank your parents for little things, and tell them you love them at unexpected times. They'll be nicer to you if they know you appreciate them.

Establish honesty and communication with your parents. And when you ask for things, ask calmly—display your maturity, set out the reasons why you should be allowed to do the things you want to do, and have a less risqué plan B for if they say no! Be ready to negotiate.

Friends are one of the best things about life.

So is Monopoly.

Life's full of open doors!

And that's all. For now. =] xx

ten toptips about inner health

Year in, year out, guys vote 'confidence' the sexiest trait a girl can have. Being insecure is, in a way, very self-centred. Accept who you are, because nobody can love you until you (honestly!) love yourself!

Next time you find yourself hunting around for a snack, ask yourself 'Am I really hungry?' You could be bored, upset or following routine. If you can't decide, have a glass of water and see if the 'hunger' passes.

It's okay to have a night in. Don't push yourself so much that you end up exhausted. There's nothing wrong with a Friday night at home, on the couch, watching a movie with your parents. No harm in chilling out!

If you employ the 'get over it' method, your friends will notice your newfound strength and ask you how you do it. Take this opportunity to explain how annoying endless whingeing is, and maybe they'll catch on.

If all you can think about is school, make some plans for the holidays. Write a list of things you want to do when you graduate, such as travel, go to uni, or get a job—it'll give you perspective and help to remind you that there really is life after school!

Your god is your god. Anyone with true faith shouldn't feel the need to try to convert others—remember that, and if someone tries to convert you, stand firm. Share your beliefs but don't force them on people.

You don't need to leave your bedroom to get exercise! Pump up the volume and dance or do aerobic exercises for a song or two. It's a fun workout and you'll barely feel like you've been exercising.

If you find yourself stressing too much about high school, spend some time on yourself. Go for a long walk, get a massage, meditate, or even just take the dog out for a bit. Take time to clear your mind.

Sometimes, for no reason at all, you may want to just sit in your room for hours and cry. That's okay—do it! You don't need an excuse and you aren't weak. And once the tears are gone you'll feel much better.

One of the best things you can do is not take anything personally. Remember that everybody's in their own world, and their view of you might be nowhere near the truth. Accept that everyone's entitled to their thoughts, but you don't have to believe them!

'The wisest thing I learnt this year was to **think before you speak.** And while I'm still implementing that in my everyday routine, the advice that's helped me the most this year is to **keep things in perspective**. Remember you're still just a kid, remember things that feel awful today will be better in a month's time, remember we all make mistakes. Remember it's okay to be wrong, and healthy to apologise. Remember we're all just getting through life as best we can. Remember not to take things too personally. **Remember to laugh at yourself.** Don't take it all to heart.'

- part of a New Year's Eve post at the end of 2009.

How old are you? 14
What do you want to be when you leave school? I want to be a designer, I really enjoy it.
Why did you want to model for this book? Mostly for the experience, and to make friends.
What's your favourite thing about yourself, and why? I like my red hair, because it's rare.
What is your most embarrassing high school memory? Going to school on a pupil free day!
If you could give the readers only one tip about surviving high school, what would it be? Don't annoy your teachers!
What's your best confidence tip? Just don't worry about what other people are thinking. That's their problem!
What achievement in your life are you most proud of? Learning how to read.

andy

anna

How old are you? 13
What do you want to be when you leave school? I hope to become a professional dancer with a great company, or just do anything to do with dancing!
What's your favourite thing about yourself, and why? I like that I am flexible, I can do the splits on all three sides!
If you could give the readers only one tip about surviving high school, what would it be? Year 7 is the worst year of high school, and after that it gets better! So don't stress if at first high school seems like the worst thing in the world :)
What achievement in your life are you most proud of? I am proud of some dancing things, but mainly proud of staying in touch with my friends from when I was little. I hope we all stay in touch forever!

How old are you? 16
What do you want to be when you leave school?
I'd like to be a music writer/composer/producer
because music is my passion and my life!
Why did you want to model for this book? To
help my friend out and try something new.
What's your favourite thing about yourself? I like
how I can make friends easily and help my friends
with any issues.
What's your best confidence tip? Always be
positive, because constantly being negative makes
you ugly inside and out.
**What achievement in your life are you most
proud of?** It's hard to answer this one because
there are many fantastic moments in life that I'm
proud of. Damn, I feel like Oprah now!

blake

cara

How old are you? 17
What do you want to be when you leave school? I
want to be an actress because I love performing.
Why did you want to model for this book? To have
a new experience and have something new to put on
my resume.
**What's your favourite thing about yourself, and
why?** My eyes, because they're big.
What's your best confidence tip? Just be yourself!
**If you could give the readers only one tip about
surviving high school, what would it be?** Work hard
and have fun!
**Has modelling for the Guide been a good
experience for you?** It's been a great experience! I'd
definitely do it again.

147

about the models

How old are you? 15

What do you want to be when you leave school? I would love to do set design or costume design—something in art.

What achievement in your life are you most proud of? I am most proud of my growth in confidence. I used to be painfully shy but I've grown out of that now :)

If you could give the readers only one tip about surviving high school, what would it be? Choose your friends wisely—don't try and 'fit in' with the bad group—at the same time don't be too picky, if there is someone in the group who you don't really like, just ignore them.

caroline

chané

How old are you? 16

What do you want to be when you leave school? I want to work with animals :D

Why did you want to model for this book? I thought it would be a good experience, and to try new things.

What's your favourite thing about yourself? My hair.

What's your best confidence tip? To just believe in yourself, because you can do whatever you put your mind to!

If you could give the readers only one tip about surviving high school, what would it be? To be yourself and to not care what others think.

If you had a million dollars and one day to spend it, what would you do with it? Buy HEAPS of clothes! :)

How old are you? 14
What do you want to be when you leave school? To be an actress; it's been my dream since I was a little girl.
What's your favourite thing about yourself? Being loud, because it helps me make friends and everyone needs a loud friend!
What achievement in your life are you most proud of? My great group of friends, who aren't afraid of being themselves and aren't trying to grow up too quickly.
What's your best confidence tip? Smile at yourself in the mirror, it makes you happier.
If you could give the readers only one tip about surviving high school, what would it be? Do your assignments on time! Pulling an all-nighter the night before is the worst.

georgia a

How old are you? 15
What do you want to be when you leave school? I want to be a vet, or get into legal or business studies.
What achievement in your life are you most proud of? Doing well at school, and learning to accept myself for who I am, flaws and all.
What's your best confidence tip? Find one part of yourself you love, remind yourself of it when you're feeling down. Eventually you will love every part of yourself.
If you could give the readers only one tip about surviving high school, what would it be? It doesn't last forever so if it's hard, hang in there and eventually it'll get better. And don't change for others!

georgia s

How old are you? 16

What do you want to do when you leave school?
A primary school teacher; I enjoy helping others and
working with kids.

**What's your most embarrassing high school
memory?** Walking into a pole whilst talking to
someone.

**If you could give the readers only one tip about
surviving high school, what would it be?** No one
knows exactly what you are going through, so don't
let your opinions influence your decisions. You can't
please everyone, so you might as well please yourself!

What achievement are you most proud of? Good
academic results at a very competitive school.

What's your best confidence tip? If you like yourself,
others will like you too.

harriet

kelli

How old are you? 17

What do you want to do when you leave school? I
have already left school and I still have absolutely no
idea!

What's your best confidence tip? Stand by what you
believe in and you will feel more confident in yourself.

**If you had a million dollars and one day to spend it,
what would you do with it?** A car, a few investment
properties, and clothes ...

**Has modelling for this book been a good
experience for you? Would you model again?**
Sure—I have done some modelling previously, and it's
always great to work with different people.

What achievement are you most proud of? Life has
only just begun—haven't done much yet!

150

How old are you? 16
What do you want to do when you leave school? Something in the performing arts, because I love dance and drama, and they're so much fun.
Why did you want to model for this book? To show people that you don't have to be 100% perfect to be a model, to boost my confidence, and to have fun.
What's your favourite thing about yourself? I think I'm a really easy, fun person to get along with, and I'm always there when someone is sad.
What is your most embarrassing high school memory? Calling a teacher 'Mum'!
What's your best confidence tip? Don't be scared to show off your talents, no matter how strange they might be!

lucy

phil

How old are you? 16
What do you want to do when you leave school? Something involving computers because I enjoy working with them.
What's your favourite thing about yourself? My sense of humour.
If you had a million dollars and one day to spend it, what would you do with it? Buy my own place, gaming equipment, car, pay my parents' debts, pool, spa, rollercoaster ... and a dog!
What achievement are you most proud of? Being called up to play football for a different team, winning the game for the finals and getting a gold medal for it.

151

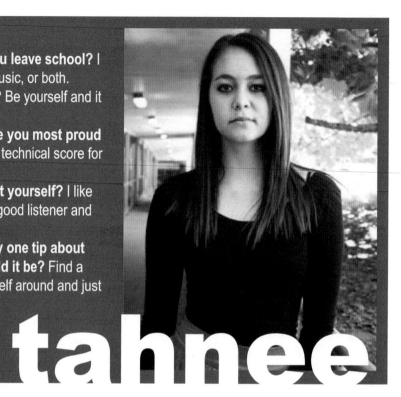

How old are you? 16
What do you want to do when you leave school? I want to do something in fashion, music, or both.
What's your best confidence tip? Be yourself and it will come naturally.
What achievement in your life are you most proud of? Winning first place and highest technical score for a fashion design competition.
What's your favourite thing about yourself? I like my sense of style and I think I'm a good listener and advice giver.
If you could give the readers only one tip about surviving high school, what would it be? Find a group of friends who you feel yourself around and just go with the flow.

tahnee

tara

How old are you? 16
What do you want to be when you leave school? Not sure yet, maybe something to do with music and journalism.
What's your favourite thing about yourself? My taste in music.
Why did you want to model for this book? To try something different and to experience new things.
What achievement in your life are you most proud of? That I got into State for tennis.
If you could give the readers only one tip about surviving high school, what would it be? Be yourself. Don't listen to those mean high school girls/boys if they're putting you down. Be the best that you can be.

Jasmine is a makeup artist in training, and she will soon be studying for her Diploma at ACMUSE (Australian College of Make Up and Special Effects). Jasmine designed and completed the makeup for all models on all three of the photo shoots, with little direction and no supervision. A huge responsibility, but we were thrilled with the outcome.

Jasmine and her wonderful mother Ansuvana also modelled for the 'You and your Parents' article, in between doing the makeup of the models that morning!

makeup artist
jasmine

153

A huge thanks to all our models and our makeup artist. These teenagers took time out of their weekends to wait around for photos and freeze in the cold! Their gorgeous faces and infectious enthusiasm were perfect for this book. If you wish to hire any of these models or the makeup artist, just visit http://www.thehighschoolsurvivalguide.com.au to request contact details.

about the authors

I'm Alex (Ally!) Mosher, 19, and fresh out of high school, which is exactly why I decided to write this book.

My story is outrageously normal—I'm a typical teenager, not amazingly popular but social enough, who grew up in the beautiful Blue Mountains (in NSW, Australia) and went to a local primary and high school. Neither of my schools were rich but we had great teachers and I enjoyed myself.

I wrote this book because all through high school I wished I had one like it. I often wrote my own ideas down because in high school, you're learning so many life lessons all at once and it's easy to make the same mistakes over again because there's just so much going on. I started blogging on MySpace and when I wrote The Myth of Popularity, a few very kind girls from younger years said they really found it helpful and subscribed to my blog. It all developed from there. I'm no expert, but I've learnt my lessons like anybody else and I want to share what I know now. Things like how important it is to be yourself. How little it matters what somebody thinks of you. Why you shouldn't worry about being cool, and why it's worth that extra hour of study each week. If I can help girls currently in high school get to know themselves better than a lot of teenagers do, my job is done.

I can be contacted through the book's website: http://www.thehighschoolsurvivalguide.com.au—I'm always happy to have a chat or answer a question!

Darren Phillips is the owner of darphi images, an accomplished photographer and short film creator ... when he's not working at a supermarket!

Darren formed darphi images in 2000. What started as a hobby for photography soon turned into a multi layered creative outlet, which covers everything from photography, filmmaking, editing, song writing and CD producing. Darren's first feature film—the rock musical Tomorrow Starts Tonight—has just been completed and is currently seeking distribution.

Having worked with Ally several times before, Darren was thrilled to be invited to be a part of this book, and found the experience very rewarding.

For more information or contact details go to www.darphiimages.net.

about the authors

Ben 'R-Tizt' Francis has contributed the male opinion throughout the book. His involvement first came about with his awesome 'mufti day' story (in The Myth of Popularity) and he's been contributing from London since then.

Ben's been performing for four years; his first performance was in front of 32 thousand people, at the age of 14. He's just turned 18 and his career is getting better by the day.

Born and raised in east London, Ben never had much of a taste for school, knowing his short concentration span was lowering his grades. Instead he put that concentration span to use, working on several different talents such as singing, beatboxing, dancing and acting. Ben's career highlights include performing for Madonna, opening a show for American rapper Tyga and performing in Camden with Daniel Bedingfield. At only 18, with a resume like that, this book is hardly worth mentioning!

'I work my heart out to help others and keep people entertained ... I will never stop entertaining, as every day a new door is opening. '

Tracy Keith is the expert behind the worklife section. She generously donated time and knowledge to a complete stranger's project, and her help has been priceless.

Tracy is a self employed career and leadership coach based in Wellington, New Zealand; visit www.tmkconsulting.co.nz.

Tracy attended four high schools and six primary schools, not because she was a really bad student, but because her father was in the army and they moved approximately every two years. This meant she was regularly making new friends, joining new communities and learning to live in a world that was always changing.

As a teenager her own personal development included: being an army brat, attending a five day Outward Bound course in Singapore, attaining a yellow belt green tip in Tae Kwon Do, receiving the Chief Commissioner's Award in Girl Guides and travelling through Europe with her family living in a VW Kombi van!

What Tracy has learnt from these lessons throughout life is to ask questions, seek out opportunities and say yes when someone offers to help you. Live the life you want to live, not the one your parents or teachers think you should be living. And have fun doing it!

acknowledgements

A zillion heartfelt thanks to:

Darren Phillips of Darphi Images, for his creative photography, patience, willingness to run with someone else's impulses, and endless supply of brilliant advice.

Tracy Keith and **Ben Francis** for their amazing input and enthusiasm.

Jennifer Mosher, my mother and publisher, for snatching up the publishing rights before I'd even finished a chapter, and for patient support and assistance since then.

The **Mosher** family, for being awesome, and **Clint Taylor,** for endless support, stress relief, and knowing when to politely nod along when I talked too much about margins and printing.

Leah Courtney, for countless reads and re-reads, and for endless help with design choices!

Paul Phillips, for being my one-man marketing department out of the kindness of his heart.

Rosie Morris, who helped cast the models and gave valuable advice throughout the process. When she's a famous model—and she will be!—I'll be proud to have known her!

Jen Jackson, who helped at the first shoot, was amazingly helpful in planning the launch, and who patiently listened to my rambling about the book for many months.

The lovely ladies at **Kingswood TAFE** for styling the girls' hair on the first shoot.

Jasmine Lovelock-Dorfler, her lovely mother **Ansuvana Lovelock**, and their gorgeous dog, for all their help and for Jasmine's fantastic make-up on the girls. Jasmine and Ansuvana are featured in the gorgeous mother-daughter portraits in the home life section.

All the fantastic **models,** guys and girls alike, for their patience, enthusiasm and willingness to be just a little bit cheesy! **Andrew, Anna, Blake, Cara, Caroline, Chané, Georgia A, Georgia S, Harriet, Kelli, Lucy, Phil, Tahnee** and **Tara**—all seriously wonderful people.

And YOU—for buying this book!

There's not much in this book that your daughter won't learn in early high school. The only topics that she might be coming across for the first time are articles such as the ones on self confidence, and the work life section. Nearly everything else can be learnt through earnest playground discussion or in class.

You might ask what the point of this book is, then, if it's all the same information they're going to get from the playground or classroom. As a parent or guardian, you probably know that children don't absorb everything that's taught to them in class, and they often don't believe what adults tell them (such as the tried-and-true 'be yourself'), dismissing it as the dated advice of an older generation, and not applicable in today's fast-paced world.

Your girl will eventually learn all the truths she needs to know, but often not until she's in her twenties. **The point of this book is to bridge that gap.** It was written to take the pain out of learning. I learnt most of these truths—such as being honest—by making mistakes. And it's important for teenagers to make mistakes and learn from them; but if they can learn some truths from this book and avoid that pain, all the better!

In order to be as practical and trustworthy as possible, this book speaks directly to your daughter—it's not patronising, and we've aimed for it to read like friends talking to one another. I especially wanted this book to be a trusted keepsake; to be the first port of call when something goes wrong. Because of that need for trust and connection, there's some mild language such as 'bitch' and 'hell', but nothing worse, and nothing they won't hear at school or on TV.

The Love Life section does include articles on what happens to your body during puberty and adolescence, and it also covers sex, unplanned pregnancy and sexuality. These are all things that your girl will learn in a health class at any public school, but it aims to give them a reference on hand so that if there's something they're not sure about, they can find answers here instead of risking misinformation by asking friends or using the internet.

We suggest that you flick through this book before giving it to your girl, so you will know what she's learning from it. All the advice in this book is just that—advice—and it all aims to be positive and sensible, but unfortunately we have no control over how a reader will interpret it, so it's always best you have a quick read first, so that you can answer any questions you may be asked. And if there's anything in the book that either of you disagree with, it could help to initiate some open, honest discussion between you.

Most of this book may seem obvious, or just plain common sense to an adult, but to a young girl learning to express herself in today's increasingly social and image-based world, this guide will help ground her and remind her **what's important in life; not what people think of her, but what she thinks of herself.**

Finally, there are no religious overtones to any articles in this book. It is designed to contain advice that can be followed within any religion.

We hope your daughter enjoys this book as much as we've loved writing it!

for advice, up-to-date information, behind the scenes photos and more, visit

www.thehighschoolsurvivalguide.com.au

or find us on Facebook:
www.facebook.com/thehighschoolsurvivalguide

29605106R00094

Made in the USA
Lexington, KY
01 February 2014